Fix-It and Forget-It
Freezer to
INSTANT POT®
Simple Make-Ahead Meals

HOPE COMERFORD

Good Books

New York, New York

Good Books books may be purchased in bulk at special discounts for sales promotion, corporate gifts, fund-raising, or educational purposes. Special editions can also be created to specifications. For details, contact the Special Sales Department, Good Books, 307 West 36th Street, 11th Floor, New York, NY 10018 or info@skyhorsepublishing.com.

Good Books is an imprint of Skyhorse Publishing, Inc.®, a Delaware corporation.

Visit our website at www.goodbooks.com.

10 9 8 7 6 5 4 3 2 1

Library of Congress Cataloging-in-Publication Data is available on file.

Cover design by David Ter-Avanesyan
Cover photo by Bonnie Matthews

Print ISBN: 978-1-68099-815-3
Ebook ISBN: 978-1-68099-835-1

Printed in China

Contents

Welcome to Fix-It and Forget-It Freezer to Instant Pot

This book is designed for just about anyone; whether you're busy, you like to plan ahead, or just like things ready to go! When life gets hectic (as it often does these days), having something ready to cook immediately when you get home is a lifesaving (and a huge time-saving) hack. If you can spend a few hours occasionally assembling some Instant Pot freezer meals, the reward will far outweigh the work!

In this book, you'll find 100 freezer to Instant Pot main dish and soup recipes that you can prepare ahead of time in freezer bags and pull out of the freezer when you're ready to cook them. Yes, you read that right! You will pull these straight out of the freezer and begin cooking them in your Instant Pot from frozen!

I generally plan for two to three freezer meals each week to cook for our four-person family. You may have a larger family, so you might want to plan for more. Do what works best for your family. Prepare as many meals as you think you have time for, the money for, or that your freezer can handle. Most of the time, everything you'll need will be right in the bag, minus your cooking liquid. Sometimes you'll need a few other ingredients at cooking time or at the time of serving. Either way, those directions are noted clearly for you.

Being prepared ahead of time will give you a newfound feeling of freedom! So get preppin' and enjoy the fruits of your labor for months!

How Does This Book Work?

For every recipe in this book, you will find specific instruction on how to prepare, freeze, and then cook each recipe when it's time. Below you will find details about each of these areas.

Needed at Time of Preparation: These are the ingredients that will go into the freezer bag.

Preparation Instructions: These are the instructions you'll need to assemble the ingredients in the freezer bag. You'll notice that the preparation instructions will always tell you to remove as much air from the freezer bag as possible before sealing. There is more information on this in the next section, so keep reading.

Information for Freezer Bag: Everything below this heading will be what will occur when you are ready to cook your freezer meal and will be the information needed on your bag if you so choose. I suggest printing off the label with all freezer bag instructions by scanning the QR code next to the recipe. Your other options are to handwrite the instructions on the bag with a permanent marker, or to just write the title of the recipe and page number on the bag so you can refer back to this book at the time of cooking. Having all the recipe information affixed to the bag is incredibly convenient, so I highly suggest the first option.

- Beneath each recipe you will find serving size, cooking time, etc. Please note: Time needed for the Instant Pot to come up to pressure and time needed for the Instant Pot to release pressure are not included in the instructions. In general, when cooking most frozen meals in the Instant Pot, it may take 20–30 minutes for the Instant Pot to come up to pressure.
- Needed at Time of Cooking/Serving: These are the additional ingredients you'll need to either add to the Instant Pot at the time of cooking, at the end of cooking, or items you'll need at the time of serving.
- Instructions: These are the cooking instructions for when you're ready to cook your freezer meal.
- Serving Suggestion: Sometimes it's nice to have some suggestions on how to serve what you're cooking. You'll find these throughout the book.

A Guide to Instant Pot Freezer Meals

1. Set aside an afternoon or morning to make 10–20 meals at a time, or enough for 2–3 months. Even though it sounds like a daunting task, this book will make the process a cinch. Make a list of the recipes you want to make, then get excited! You may even consider making multiple batches of certain meals. This is going to make your life easier in the long run!
2. You will need to freeze your freezer bags in circular containers that are slightly smaller than the diameter of your Instant Pot's inner pot. Make sure you have enough of these containers on hand for your meal prepping session.
3. Make a shopping list for the recipes you're going to make. Look at all the ingredient lists for the recipes you've chosen. As you write them down, categorize your list to make shopping a breeze! I love that I can grab all the ingredients I need quickly when I'm preparing freezer meals because all of my produce, meats, seasonings,

etc. are grouped together on the list. Be sure to check in your pantry to see what you already have so you don't buy more than you need.

4. Buy precut veggies if you can. This will cut down on some of your preparation time, but probably won't save you money. I like to buy precut mushrooms because I know they take a lot of preparation and I can find them presliced easily.

5. If you can't buy or find precut veggies, save some time by using your food processor. This makes chopping all the onions *so* much easier!

6. Have a butcher prepare your meat for you. Just call ahead and let them know exactly what and how much you need. They may even give you a discount, all while preparing your meats just the way you need them.

7. Have lots of freezer bags on hand. You will need 1-gallon freezer bags for the most part for this book. I buy them in bulk so I always have plenty on hand. If you're not a freezer bag user, then use good freezer-safe containers that are circular and are slightly smaller than the diameter of your Instant Pot inner pot.

8. Make sure to label all your freezer bags or containers well. Always put the date you've prepared the bag on them so you know how long it's been in the freezer.

9. Print off the instructions by scanning the QR codes for each recipe and affix them to the bags. This will save you a lot of time and energy!

10. Help to avoid freezer burn by removing as much of the air as you can from your freezer bags. Little coffee stirrer straws can help you get most of the air out. Insert the straw in the center of the bag (being careful not to touch the raw ingredients) and while you're sucking the air out, close the bag tightly around it, then slide the straw out and finish sealing. If you have a vacuum sealer, you may even consider that route.

11. For best results, use your freezer meals up within 4–6 months of freezing.

12. To easily remove the food from the freezer bags to place them into your Instant Pot, just run some warm water over the bag for a minute or two, or until the bag pulls away from the contents inside. You could also just place the bag into a bowl of warm water while you get your Instant Pot out and set it up. Easy peasy!

What Is an Instant Pot?

In short, an Instant Pot is a digital pressure cooker that also has multiple other functions. Not only can it be used as a pressure cooker, but depending on which model Instant Pot you have, you can also set it to do things like sauté, or cook rice, multigrains, porridge, soup/stew, beans/chili, porridge, meat, poultry, cake, eggs, and make yogurt. The Instant Pot can steam, slow

cook, or even be set manually. Because the Instant Pot has so many functions, it takes away the need for multiple appliances on your counter and uses fewer pots and pans.

Getting Started with Your Instant Pot

Get to know your Instant Pot . . .

The very first thing most Instant Pot owners do is called the water test. It helps you get to know your Instant Pot a bit, familiarizes you with it, and might even take a bit of your apprehension away (because if you're anything like me, I was scared to death to use it!).

Step 1: Plug in your Instant Pot. This may seem obvious to some, but when we're nervous about using a new appliance, sometimes we forget things like this.

Step 2: Make sure the inner pot is inserted in the cooker. You should NEVER attempt to cook anything in your device without the inner pot, or you will ruin your Instant Pot. Food should never come into contact with the actual housing unit.

Step 3: The inner pot has lines for each cup (how convenient, right?!). Fill the inner pot with water until it reaches the 3-cup line.

Step 4: Check the sealing ring to be sure it's secure and in place. You should not be able to move it around. If it's not in place properly, you may experience issues with the pot letting out a lot of steam while cooking, or not coming to pressure.

Step 5: Seal the lid. There is an arrow on the lid between "open" and "close." There is also an arrow on the top of the base of the Instant Pot between a picture of a locked lock and an unlocked lock. Line those arrows up, then turn the lid toward the picture of the lock (left). You will hear a noise that will indicate the lid is locked. If you do not hear a noise, it's not locked. Try it again.

Step 6: ALWAYS check to see if the steam valve on top of the lid is turned to "sealing." If it's not on "sealing" and is on "venting," it will not be able to come to pressure.

Step 7: Press the "Steam" button and use the +/- arrow to set it to 2 minutes. Once it's at the desired time, you don't need to press anything else. In a few seconds, the Instant Pot will begin all on its own. For those of us with digital slow cookers, we have a tendency to look for the "start" button, but there isn't one on the Instant Pot.

Step 8: Now you wait for the "magic" to happen! The "cooking" will begin once the device comes to pressure. This can take anywhere from 5 to 30 minutes, I've found in my experience. Then, you will see the countdown happen from the time at which you set it. After that, the Instant Pot will beep, which means your meal is done!

Step 9: Your Instant Pot will now automatically switch to "warm" and begin a count of how many minutes it's been on warm. The next part is where you either wait for the NPR, or natural pressure release (meaning the pressure releases all on its own), or you do what's called a QR, or quick release (meaning, you manually release the pressure). Which method you choose depends on what you're cooking, but in this case, you can choose either since it's just water. For NPR, you will wait for the lever to move all the way back over to "venting" and watch the pinion (float valve) next to the lever. It will be flush with the lid when at full pressure and will drop when the pressure is done releasing. If you choose QR, be very careful not to have your hands over the vent as the steam is very hot and you can burn yourself.

The Three Most Important Buttons You Need to Know About . . .

You will find the majority of recipes will use the following three buttons:

Manual/Pressure Cook: Some older models tend to say "Manual," and the newer models seem to say "Pressure Cook." They mean the same thing. From here, you use the +/- button to change the cook time. After several seconds, the Instant Pot will begin its process. The exact name of this button will vary on your model of Instant Pot.

Sauté: Many recipes will have you sauté vegetables or brown meat before beginning the pressure cooking process. For this setting, you will not use the lid of the Instant Pot.

Keep Warm/Cancel: This may just be the most important button on the Instant Pot. When you forget to use the +/- buttons to change the time for a recipe, or you press a wrong button, you can hit "keep warm/cancel" and it will turn your Instant Pot off for you.

What Do All the Buttons Do?

With so many buttons, it's hard to remember what each one does or means. You can use this as a quick guide in a pinch.

Soup/Broth. This button cooks at high pressure for 30 minutes. It can be adjusted using the +/- buttons to cook more for 40 minutes, or less for 20 minutes.

Meat/Stew. This button cooks at high pressure for 35 minutes. It can be adjusted using the +/- buttons to cook more for 45 minutes, or less for 20 minutes.

Bean/Chili. This button cooks at high pressure for 30 minutes. It can be adjusted using the +/- buttons to cook more for 40 minutes, or less for 25 minutes.

Poultry. This button cooks at high pressure for 15 minutes. It can be adjusted using the +/- buttons to cook more for 30 minutes, or less for 5 minutes.

Rice. This button cooks at low pressure and is the only fully automatic program. It is for cooking white rice and will automatically adjust the cooking time depending on the amount of water and rice in the cooking pot.

Multigrain. This button cooks at high pressure for 40 minutes. It can be adjusted using the +/- buttons to cook more for 45 minutes of warm water soaking time and 60 minutes pressure cooking time, or less for 20 minutes.

Porridge. This button cooks at high pressure for 20 minutes. It can be adjusted using the +/- buttons to cook more for 30 minutes, or less for 15 minutes.

Steam. This button cooks at high pressure for 10 minutes. It can be adjusted using the +/- buttons to cook more for 15 minutes, or less for 3 minutes. Always use a rack or steamer basket with this function because it heats at full power continuously while it's coming to pressure, and you do not want food in direct contact with the bottom of the pressure cooking pot or it will burn. Once it reaches pressure, the steam button regulates pressure by cycling on and off, similar to the other pressure buttons.

Less | Normal | More. Adjust between the *Less | Normal | More* settings by pressing the same cooking function button repeatedly until you get to the desired setting. (Older versions use the *Adjust* button.)

+/- Buttons. Adjust the cook time up [+] or down [-]. (On newer models, you can also press and hold [-] or [+] for 3 seconds to turn sound off or on.)

Cake. This button cooks at high pressure for 30 minutes. It can be adjusted using the +/- buttons to cook more for 40 minutes, or less for 25 minutes.

Egg. This button cooks at high pressure for 5 minutes. It can be adjusted using the +/- buttons to cook more for 6 minutes, or less for 4 minutes.

Instant Pot Tips and Tricks and Other Things You May Not Know

- Never attempt to cook directly in the Instant Pot without the inner pot!
- Once you set the time, you can walk away. It will show the time you set it to, then will change to the word "on" while the pressure builds. Once the Instant Pot has

come to pressure, you will once again see the time you set it for. It will count down from there.

- Always make sure your sealing ring is securely in place. If it shows signs of wear or tear, it needs to be replaced.
- Have a sealing ring for savory recipes and a separate sealing ring for sweet recipes. Many people report of their desserts tasting like a roast (or another savory food) if they try to use the same sealing ring for all recipes.
- The stainless steel rack (trivet) your Instant Pot comes with can be used to keep food from being completely submerged in liquid, like baked potatoes or ground beef. It can also be used to set another pot on, for pot-in-pot cooking.
- If you use warm or hot liquid instead of cold liquid, you may need to adjust the cooking time, or your food may not come out done.
- Always double-check to see that the valve on the lid is set to "sealing" and not "venting" when you first lock the lid. This will save you from your Instant Pot not coming to pressure.
- Use Natural Pressure Release for tougher cuts of meat, recipes with high starch (like rice or grains), and recipes with a high volume of liquid. This means you let the Instant Pot naturally release pressure. The little bobbin will fall once pressure is released completely.
- Use Quick Release for more delicate cuts of meat and vegetables, like seafood, chicken breasts, and steaming vegetables. This means you manually turn the vent (being careful not to put your hand over the vent!!!) to release the pressure. The little bobbin will fall once pressure is released completely.
- Make sure there is a clear pathway for the steam to release. The last thing you want is to ruin the bottom of your cupboards with all that steam.
- You MUST use liquid in your Instant Pot. The MINIMUM amount of liquid you should have in your inner pot is ½ cup; however, most recipes work best with at least 1 cup.
- Do NOT overfill your Instant Pot! It should only be ½ full for rice or beans (food that expands greatly when cooked), or ⅔ of the way full for most everything else. To be safe, do not even fill it to the max filled line.
- In this book, the cooking time DOES NOT take into account the amount of time it will take your Instant Pot to come to pressure, or the amount of time it will take the Instant Pot to release pressure. Be aware of this when choosing a recipe to make.
- If your Instant Pot is not coming to pressure, it's usually because the sealing ring is not on properly, or the vent is not set to "sealing."

- The more liquid, or the colder the ingredients, the longer it will take for the Instant Pot to come to pressure.
- Always make sure that the Instant Pot is dry before inserting the inner pot, and make sure the inner pot is dry before inserting it into the Instant Pot.
- Use a binder clip to hold the inner pot tight against the outer pot when sautéing and stirring. This will keep the pot from "spinning" in the base.
- Doubling a recipe does not change the cook time, but instead it will take longer to come up to pressure.
- You do not always need to double the liquid when doubling a recipe. Depending on what you're making, more liquid may make your food too watery. Use your best judgment.
- When using the slow cooker function, use the following chart:

Slow Cooker	Instant Pot
Warm	Less or Low
Low	Normal or Medium
High	More or High

Instant Pot Accessories

Most Instant Pots come with a stainless-steel trivet. Below, you will find a list of accessories that will be used in this cookbook. Most of these accessories can be purchased in-store or online easily from several retailers.

- Trivet and/or steamer basket—stainless steel or silicone
- 7-inch springform cake pan—nonstick or silicone 7-inch round baking pan

Freezer Meal Recipes

Chicken & Turkey
Main Dishes

Root Beer Chicken Wings

Hope Comerford, Clinton Township, MI

Makes 15–18 servings
Prep. Time: 5 minutes

Needed at Time of Preparation:

5 lb. chicken wings, tips removed and separated at joint (or 5-lb. bag of frozen chicken wings)

Note: If you are using a bag of frozen chicken wings, you can skip the preparation instructions. Leave them in the bag they came in until you are ready to use them.

Preparation Instructions:

1. On baking sheets lined with parchment paper, lay out a single layer of the trimmed chicken wings and freeze. Once frozen, place them in a freezer bag.

2. Remove as much air as possible from the freezer bag and seal it. Label the bag. Freeze.

Information for Freezer Bag:

ROOT BEER CHICKEN WINGS

Makes 6–8 servings
I.P. Cook Time: 8 minutes   Oven Cook Time: 2 minutes

Needed at Time of Cooking:

1 cup water

¼ cup root beer

¼ cup brown sugar

½ tsp. red pepper flakes

Instructions:

1. Place the trivet into the inner pot and pour in the water. Pour the wings onto the trivet and spread out as evenly as possible.

2. Secure the lid and set the vent to sealing. Manually set the cook time for 8 minutes on high pressure.

3. Preheat the oven on broil.

4. When cook time is up, let the pressure release naturally for 10 minutes, then manually release the rest of the pressure.

5. Remove the wings and spread them out on a greased baking sheet.

6. Mix together the root beer, brown sugar, and red pepper flakes. Brush this over the wings.

7. Place the wings under the broiler for 2 minutes.

Levi's Sesame Chicken Wings

Shirley Unternahrer Hinh, Wayland, IA

Makes 6 servings
Prep. Time: 5–10 minutes

Needed at Time of Preparation:

3 lb. chicken wings, tips removed and separated at joint (or 3-lb. bag of frozen chicken wings)

1 cup sugar substitute to equal 6 tablespoons sugar

¾ cup light soy sauce

½ cup no-salt-added ketchup

2 Tbsp. canola oil

2 Tbsp. sesame oil

2 cloves garlic, minced

Salt to taste

Pepper to taste

Note: If you are using a bag of frozen chicken wings, you can skip the preparation instructions. Leave them in the bag they came in until you are ready to use them.

Preparation Instructions:

1. On baking sheets lined with parchment paper, lay out a single layer of the trimmed chicken wings and freeze. Once frozen, place them in a freezer bag.

2. In a separate, smaller freezer bag, place the remaining ingredients. Seal the bag. Place this bag in the bag with the chicken wings and remove as much air as possible before sealing and labeling the bag. Freeze.

LEVI'S SESAME CHICKEN WINGS

Makes 6 servings

I.P. Cook Time: 8 minutes ❦ *Oven Cook Time: 5 minutes*

Needed at Time of Cooking:

1 cup water

Toasted sesame seeds

Instructions:

1. Place the smaller bag with the sauce ingredients into a bowl of warm water while you get the wings going in the Instant Pot.

2. Place the trivet in the Instant Pot inner pot with 1 cup of water. Carefully place the chicken wings on top of the trivet.

3. Secure the lid and make sure vent is set to sealing. Manually set the cook time for 8 minutes on high pressure.

4. Empty the contents of the smaller freezer bag into a small pot. Let it defrost completely and simmer while the wings cook.

5. When the Instant Pot cook time is up, let the pressure release naturally for 10 minutes, then manually release the remaining pressure.

6. Meanwhile, line a baking sheet with foil and place a baking rack on top. Turn the oven to broil.

7. Carefully remove about half of the wings into a bowl and pour half of the sauce over the top. Gently stir to coat them, then place them on top of the baking rack. Repeat this process with the remaining wings and sauce.

8. Broil the wings about 5 inches from the top of the oven for 5 minutes.

9. Sprinkle sesame seeds over top just before serving.

Marinated Chicken Bites

June Hackenberger, Thompsontown, PA

Makes 6–8 servings
Prep. Time: 5–10 minutes

Needed at Time of Preparation:

2 lb. boneless, skinless chicken thighs,
cut into 1½" chunks

½ cup soy sauce

¼ cup oil

¼ cup apple cider vinegar

1 tsp. oregano

½ tsp. basil

¼ tsp. garlic powder

¼ tsp. parsley

¼ tsp. black pepper

Preparation Instructions:

1. Combine all ingredients in a freezer bag. Smoosh around to combine.

2. Seal the bag, removing as much air as possible, then label it.

3. Place the freezer bag into a circular container that is slightly smaller than the diameter of your Instant Pot inner pot and freeze.

Information for Freezer Bag:

MARINATED CHICKEN BITES

Makes 6–8 servings
Cook Time: 10 minutes

Needed at Time of Cooking:

½ cup water

½ cup chicken stock

Serving Suggestion: Serve with garlic bread and salad.

Instructions:

1. Place the water, chicken stock, and contents of bag into the inner pot of the Instant Pot.

2. Secure the lid and set the vent to sealing. Manually set the cook time to 10 minutes on high pressure.

3. When cook time is up, let the pressure release naturally for 5 minutes, then manually release the remaining pressure.

Greek Chicken

Judy Govotsos, Monrovia, MD

Makes 6 servings
Prep. Time: 10 minutes

Needed at Time of Preparation:

2 lb. boneless, skinless chicken thighs cut into 1½" pieces

2 large onions, quartered

6–8 cloves garlic, minced

3 tsp. dried oregano

¾ tsp. salt

½ tsp. pepper

Preparation Instructions:

1. Place all ingredients in a freezer bag.

2. Seal the bag and remove as much air as possible, then label it.

3. Place the freezer bag into a circular container that is slightly smaller than the diameter of your Instant Pot inner pot and freeze.

Information for Freezer Bag:

GREEK CHICKEN

Makes 6 servings
Cook Time: 20 minutes

Needed at Time of Cooking:

4 potatoes, peeled, chopped into 1" cubes

1 Tbsp. olive oil

1 cup chicken stock

Serving Suggestion: Serve with a Greek salad.

Instructions:

1. Place the potatoes, oil, chicken stock, and contents of the bag into the inner pot of the Instant Pot.

2. Secure the lid and make sure vent is set to sealing. Manually set cook time for 10 minutes on high pressure.

3. When cook time is over, let the pressure release naturally for 10 minutes, then release the rest manually.

Butter Chicken

Jessica Stoner, Arlington, OH

Makes 4 servings
Prep. Time: 10 minutes

Needed at Time of Preparation:

2 lb. boneless, skinless chicken thighs, cut into 1½" pieces

1 medium onion, chopped

1–2 medium cloves garlic, minced

½ Tbsp. minced ginger

1 tsp. garam masala

½ tsp. turmeric

2 tsp. kosher salt

¼ cup tomato paste

2 cups crushed tomatoes

1½ Tbsp. honey

Preparation Instructions:

1. Place all ingredients in a freezer bag.

2. Seal the bag, removing as much air as possible, then label it.

3. Place the freezer bag into a circular container that is slightly smaller than the diameter of your Instant Pot inner pot and freeze.

Information for Freezer Bag:

BUTTER CHICKEN

Makes 4 servings
Cook Time: 10 minutes

Needed at Time of Cooking:

1 cup chicken stock

1½ cups heavy cream

1 Tbsp. butter

Serving Suggestion: Serve with basmati rice and naan.

Instructions:

1. Place the chicken stock and contents of the freezer bag into the inner pot of the Instant Pot.

2. Secure the lid and make sure the vent is set to sealing. Set the cook time for 10 minutes on high pressure.

3. When cook time is up, let the pressure release naturally for 10 minutes, then manually release the remaining pressure.

4. Remove the lid and change to the Sauté function. Slowly stir in the heavy cream and bring to a simmer. Simmer for 5 minutes. Stir in the butter until melted and turn off.

Garlic Galore Chicken

Hope Comerford, Clinton Township, MI

Makes 4 servings
Prep. Time: 5 minutes

Needed at Time of Preparation:

2 lb. boneless, skinless chicken thighs, cut into 1½" pieces

Salt to taste

Pepper to taste

20–30 cloves fresh garlic, peeled and left whole

2 Tbsp. garlic powder

2 tsp. onion powder

½ tsp. basil

½ tsp. cumin

½ tsp. chili powder

Preparation Instructions:

1. Place all the ingredients in a freezer bag and smoosh around.

2. Seal the bag, removing as much air as possible, then label it.

3. Place the freezer bag into a circular container that is slightly smaller than the diameter of your Instant Pot inner pot and freeze.

Information for Freezer Bag:

GARLIC GALORE CHICKEN

Makes 4 servings
Cook Time: 10 minutes

Needed at Time of Cooking:

1 cup chicken stock

Serving Suggestion: Serve with rice and a vegetable of your choice.

Instructions:

1. Place the chicken stock and contents of the freezer bag into the inner pot of the Instant Pot.

2. Secure the lid and set the vent to sealing. Manually set the cook time for 10 minutes on high pressure.

3. When cook time is up, let the pressure release naturally for 10 minutes, then manually release the remaining pressure.

Chicken in Mushroom Gravy

Rosemarie Fitzgerald, Gibsonia, PA
Audrey L. Kneer, Williamsfield, IL

Makes 6 servings
Prep. Time: 10 minutes

Needed at Time of Preparation:

6 (5-oz. each) boneless, skinless
chicken-breast halves, cut into 1½"
pieces

Salt to taste

Pepper to taste

4 oz, sliced mushrooms

10¾-oz. can condensed cream of
mushroom soup

Preparation Instructions:

1. Place all the ingredients in a freezer bag. Smoosh around.

2. Seal the bag, removing as much air as possible, then label it.

3. Place the freezer bag into a circular container that is slightly smaller than the diameter of your Instant Pot inner pot and freeze.

Information for Freezer Bag:

CHICKEN IN MUSHROOM GRAVY

Makes 6 servings
Cook Time: 10 minutes

Needed at Time of Cooking:

½ cup dry white wine

½ cup chicken broth

Serving Suggestion: Serve
over egg noodles or your
favorite pasta.

Instructions:

1. Place the wine, chicken broth, and contents of the freezer bag into the inner pot of Instant Pot.

2. Secure the lid and make sure the vent is set to sealing. Manually set the cook time for 10 minutes on high pressure.

3. When the cook time is up, let the pressure release naturally for 5 minutes, then manually release the remaining pressure.

Chicken with Spiced Sesame Sauce

Colleen Heatwole, Burton, MI

Makes 4–6 servings
Prep. Time: 10 minutes

Needed at Time of Preparation:

2 lb. boneless, skinless chicken thighs, cut into 1½" pieces

2 Tbsp. tahini (sesame sauce)

1 Tbsp. soy sauce

¼ cup chopped onion

1 tsp. red wine vinegar

2 tsp. minced garlic

1 tsp. shredded ginger root (Microplane works best)

Preparation Instructions:

1. Place all ingredients in a freezer bag.

2. Seal the bag, removing as much air as possible, then label it.

3. Place the freezer bag into a circular container that is slightly smaller than the diameter of your Instant Pot inner pot and freeze.

Information for Freezer Bag:

CHICKEN WITH SPICED SESAME SAUCE

Makes 4–6 servings
Cook Time: 10 minutes

Needed at Time of Cooking:
1 cup chicken broth

Needed at Time of Serving:
Sandwich buns for 4–6 people

Instructions:

1. Place the chicken broth and contents of the freezer bag into the inner pot of the Instant Pot.

2. Secure the lid and set the vent to sealing. Manually set the cook for 10 minutes on high pressure.

3. When cook time is up, let the pressure release naturally for 10 minutes, then manually release the remaining pressure.

4. Remove the chicken and shred chicken with forks. Combine with the other ingredients in the pot for a tasty sandwich filling.

Chicken Dinner in a Packet

Bonnie Whaling, Clearfield, PA

Makes 4 servings
Prep. Time: 10 minutes

Needed at Time of Preparation:

2 lb. boneless, skinless chicken breasts

2 cups sliced fresh mushrooms

2 medium carrots, cut into 2" chunks

1 medium zucchini, cut into 2" chunks

2 Tbsp. olive, or canola, oil

2 Tbsp. lemon juice

1 Tbsp. fresh basil, or 1 tsp. dry basil

¼ tsp. salt

¼ tsp. black pepper

Preparation Instructions:

1. Fold four 12" × 28" pieces of foil in half to make four 12" × 14" rectangles. Divide the chicken evenly between each piece of foil.

2. Divide the mushrooms, carrots, and zucchini equally between chicken bundles.

3. In a small bowl, stir together oil, lemon juice, basil, salt, and pepper. Drizzle the mixture equally between the packets.

4. Pull up two opposite edges of foil. Seal with a double fold. Then fold in remaining edges, leaving enough space for steam to build during cook time.

5. Place the 4 foil packets in a freezer bag, removing as much air as possible, then label it. Freeze.

Information for Freezer Bag:

CHICKEN DINNER IN A PACKET

Makes 4 servings
Cook Time: 8 minutes

Needed at Time of Cooking:

1 cup water

Instructions:

1. Pour 1 cup of water into the inner pot of the Instant Pot and place the trivet or a steamer basket on top.

2. Place the bundles from the freezer bag on top of the trivet, or inside the steamer basket.

3. Secure the lid and set the vent to sealing. Manually set the cook time for 8 minutes at high pressure.

4. When cook time is up, let the pressure release naturally for 10 minutes, then manually release the remaining pressure.

Pineapple Chicken

Amanda Gross, Souderton, PA

Makes 3–4 servings
Prep. Time: 5 minutes

Needed at Time of Preparation:

4 boneless, skinless chicken thighs, cut into 1½" pieces

¼ cup soy sauce

½ cup pineapple juice

½ cup ketchup

2 Tbsp. white vinegar

16-oz. can crushed pineapple

Preparation Instructions:

1. Place all ingredients in a freezer bag.

2. Seal the bag, removing as much air as possible, then label it.

3. Place the freezer bag into a circular container that is slightly smaller than the diameter of your Instant Pot inner pot and freeze.

Information for Freezer Bag:

PINEAPPLE CHICKEN

Makes 3–4 servings
Cook Time: 10 minutes

Needed at Time of Cooking:

1 cup chicken stock or water

Serving Suggestion: Serve over cooked rice.

Instructions:

1. Pour the chicken stock or water, along with the contents of the freezer bag, into the inner pot of the Instant Pot.

2. Secure the lid and set the vent to sealing. Manually set the cook time for 10 minutes on high pressure.

3. When cook time is up, let the pressure release naturally for 10 minutes, then manually release the remaining pressure.

Cranberry Chili Chicken

Kelly Bailey, Mechanicsburg, PA

Makes 6 servings
Prep. Time: 10 minutes

Needed at Time of Preparation:

6 boneless, skinless chicken thighs, cut into 1½" pieces

½ cup chili sauce

2 Tbsp. orange marmalade

½ cup whole-berry cranberry sauce

¼ tsp. ground allspice

Preparation Instructions:

1. Place all ingredients in a freezer bag and smoosh everything around.

2. Seal the bag, removing as much air as possible, then label it.

3. Place the freezer bag into a circular container that is slightly smaller than the diameter of your Instant Pot inner pot and freeze.

Information for Freezer Bag:

CRANBERRY CHILI CHICKEN

Makes 6 servings
Cook Time: 10 minutes

Needed at Time of Cooking:

1 cup chicken stock

Serving Suggestion: Serve with mashed potatoes and a vegetable of your choice.

Instructions:

1. Place the chicken stock and the contents of the freezer bag into the inner pot of the Instant Pot.

2. Secure the lid and set the vent to sealing. Manually set the cook time for 10 minutes on high pressure.

3. When cook time is up, let the pressure release naturally for 10 minutes, then manually release the remaining pressure.

4. Serve the chicken topped with the sauce.

Mild Chicken Curry with Coconut Milk

Brittney Horst, Lititz, PA

Makes 4–6 servings
Prep. Time: 10 minutes

Needed at Time of Preparation:

4 lb. boneless, skinless chicken thighs, cut into 1½" pieces

1 large onion, chopped

6 cloves garlic, crushed

½ tsp. black pepper

½ tsp. turmeric

½ tsp. paprika

¼ tsp. cinnamon

¼ tsp. cloves

¼ tsp. cumin

¼ tsp. ginger

½ tsp. salt

1 Tbsp. curry powder (more if you like more flavor)

½ tsp. chili powder

24-oz. can diced or crushed tomatoes

Preparation Instructions:

1. Place all ingredients in a freezer bag and smoosh around.

2. Seal the bag, removing as much air as possible, then label it.

3. Place the freezer bag into a circular container that is slightly smaller than the diameter of your Instant Pot inner pot and freeze.

MILD CHICKEN CURRY WITH COCONUT MILK

Makes 4–6 servings

Cook Time: 10 minutes

Needed at Time of Cooking:

13½-oz. can of coconut milk

Serving suggestion: Serve on rice, with a vegetable of your choice on the side.

Instructions:

1. Pour the coconut milk into the inner pot and then empty the contents of the freezer bag into the milk.

2. Secure the lid and set the vent to sealing. Manually set the cook time for 10 minutes on high pressure.

3. When the cook time is up, let the pressure release naturally for 10 minutes, then manually release the remaining pressure.

Chicken with Lemon

Colleen Heatwole, Burton, MI

Makes 4 servings
Prep. Time: 10 minutes

Needed at Time of Preparation:

1 lemon, organic preferred

2 lb. boneless, skinless chicken thighs,
cut into 1 ½" pieces

1 Tbsp. olive oil

1 tsp. rosemary

1 tsp. kosher salt

½ tsp. black pepper

1 medium onion, chopped

2 cloves garlic, minced

Preparation Instructions:

1. Wash lemon, trim ends, quarter lengthwise, and remove seeds. Slice quarters crosswise into ⅛" slices.

2. Place the lemons and remaining ingredients in a freezer bag and smoosh around.

3. Seal the bag, removing as much air as possible, then label it.

4. Place the freezer bag into a circular container that is slightly smaller than the diameter of your Instant Pot inner pot and freeze.

Information for Freezer Bag:

CHICKEN WITH LEMON

Makes 4 servings
Cook Time: 10 minutes

Needed at Time of Cooking:

1 cup chicken stock

Serving Suggestion: Serve with a salad.

Instructions:

1. Pour the stock and contents of the freezer bag into the inner pot of the Instant Pot.

2. Secure the lid and set vent to sealing. Manually set the cook time to 10 minutes on high pressure.

3. When cook time is up, allow the pressure to release naturally for 10 minutes, then manually release the remaining pressure.

Orange Chicken

Anita Troyer, Fairview, MI

Makes 6 servings
Prep. Time: 10 minutes

Needed at Time of Preparation:

2 lb. boneless, skinless chicken breasts, cut into 1½" pieces

1 Tbsp. grated fresh ginger

4 cloves garlic, minced

1 Tbsp. rice wine

½ cup tomato sauce

⅓ cup brown sugar

¼ cup soy sauce

Zest of 1 orange

Preparation Instructions:

1. Place all ingredients in a freezer bag and mush around. Seal the bag, removing as much air as possible, then label it.

2. Place the freezer bag into a circular container that is slightly smaller than the diameter of your Instant Pot inner pot and freeze.

Information for Freezer Bag:

ORANGE CHICKEN

Makes 6 servings
Cook Time: 10 minutes

Needed at Time of Cooking:

1 cup orange juice plus 2 Tbsp. orange juice, divided

2 Tbsp. cornstarch

Serving Suggestion: Serve over cooked rice.

Instructions:

1. Pour 1 cup of orange juice and the contents of the freezer bag into the inner pot of the Instant Pot.

2. Secure the lid and set the vent to sealing. Manually set the cook time for 10 minutes on high pressure.

3. When cook time is up, let the pressure release naturally for 10 minutes, then manually release the remaining pressure.

4. Remove the lid and turn pot to Sauté.

5. Combine the 2 Tbsp. of orange juice and cornstarch in a small bowl and stir until well mixed. Add to the pot and gently stir to combine. If stirred too vigorously, the chicken will fall apart.

6. Keep on Sauté setting until thickened, 2–3 minutes. Turn pot off by pressing Cancel.

BBQ Chicken Sandwiches

Sarah Herr, Goshen, IN

Makes 8 servings
Prep. Time: 15 minutes

Needed at Time of Preparation:

3 lb. boneless, skinless chicken thighs, cut into 1½" pieces

1 onion, chopped

½ cup brown sugar

½ cup apple cider vinegar

½ cup ketchup

1 tsp. ground mustard

1 tsp. cumin

1 Tbsp. chili powder

½ tsp. black pepper

Preparation Instructions:

1. Place all ingredients in a freezer bag and smoosh around.

2. Seal the bag, removing as much air as possible, then label it.

3. Place the freezer bag into a circular container that is slightly smaller than the diameter of your Instant Pot inner pot and freeze.

Information for Freezer Bag:

BBQ CHICKEN SANDWICHES

Makes 8 servings
Cook Time: 10 minutes

Needed at Time of Cooking/ Serving:

½ cup apple juice

½ cup chicken stock

8 hamburger buns

Instructions:

1. Pour the apple juice, chicken stock, and contents of the freezer bag into the inner pot of the Instant Pot.

2. Secure the lid and set the vent to sealing. Manually set the cook time for 10 minutes on high pressure.

3. When cook time is up, let the pressure release naturally for 10 minutes, then manually release the remaining pressure.

4. Lift cooked chicken out of the inner pot and shred with two forks.

5. Stir the shredded meat back into sauce in inner pot.

6. Serve on the hamburger buns.

Chicken Cacciatore with Vegetables

Marla Folkerts, Batavia, IL

Makes 4 servings
Prep. Time: 10 minutes

Needed at Time of Preparation:

2 lb. boneless, skinless chicken thighs, chopped into 1½" pieces

28-oz. can diced tomatoes

½ red bell pepper and ½ green bell pepper, cut lengthwise

½ large onion, chopped

1 tsp. dried oregano

1 bay leaf

Salt to taste

Pepper to taste

1-lb. bag baby carrots

Preparation Instructions:

1. Place all ingredients in a freezer bag and smoosh around so everything is evenly coated.

2. Seal the bag, removing as much air as possible, then label it.

3. Place the freezer bag into a circular container that is slightly smaller than the diameter of your Instant Pot inner pot and freeze.

Information for Freezer Bag:

CHICKEN CACCIATORE WITH VEGETABLES

Makes 4 servings
Cook Time: 10 Minutes

Needed at Time of Cooking:

3–4 large potatoes, washed, peeled, and chopped into 1½" chunks

1 cup chicken stock

Instructions:

1. Place potatoes, chicken stock, and contents the of freezer bag into the inner pot of the Instant Pot.

2. Secure the lid and set the vent to sealing. Manually set the cook time for 10 minutes on high pressure.

3. When cook time is up, let the pressure release naturally for 10 minutes, then manually release the remaining pressure.

4. Remove the bay leaf before serving.

Creamy Italian Chicken

Amanda Gross, Souderton, PA

Makes 4 servings
Prep. Time: 5 minutes

Needed at Time of Preparation:

2 lb. boneless, skinless chicken thighs, cut into 1½" pieces

10¾-oz. can cream of chicken condensed soup

1 oz. dry Italian dressing spices

Preparation Instructions:

1. Place all ingredients in a freezer bag and smoosh around.

2. Seal the bag, removing as much air as possible, then label it.

3. Place the freezer bag into a circular container that is slightly smaller than the diameter of your Instant Pot inner pot and freeze.

Information for Freezer Bag:

CREAMY ITALIAN CHICKEN

Makes 4 servings
Cook Time: 10 minutes

Needed at Time of Cooking:

1 cup chicken stock

8-oz. brick cream cheese, cut into 1" chunks and at room temperature

Serving Suggestion: Serve over cooked noodles.

Instructions:

1. Pour the chicken stock and contents of the freezer bag into the inner pot of the Instant Pot.

2. Secure the lid and set the vent to sealing. Manually set the cook time for 10 minutes on high pressure.

3. When cook time is up, let the pressure release naturally for 10 minutes, then manually release the remaining pressure.

4. Set the pot to Sauté and add the cream cheese. Stir gently until is is completely melted in.

Italian Chicken and Broccoli

Liz Clapper, Lancaster, PA

Makes 6 servings
Prep. Time: 15 minutes

Needed at Time of Preparation:

1 lb. boneless, skinless chicken thighs,
cut into 1" strips

1 head broccoli, chopped into florets
(about 4 cups)

2 cloves garlic, finely chopped

4 medium carrots, sliced into 1" chunks

1 Tbsp. olive oil

1½ Tbsp. Italian seasoning

Preparation Instructions:

1. Place all ingredients in a freezer bag and smoosh around.

2. Seal the bag, removing as much air as possible, then label it.

3. Place the freezer bag into a circular container that is slightly smaller than the diameter of your Instant Pot inner pot and freeze.

Information for Freezer Bag:

ITALIAN CHICKEN AND BROCCOLI

Makes 6 servings
Cook Time: 10 minutes

Needed at Time of Cooking/ Serving:

3 cups chicken broth

2 cups uncooked macaroni pasta, cooked according to package instructions

¼ cup shredded Parmesan cheese

Instructions:

1. Pour the chicken broth and contents of the freezer bag into the inner pot of the Instant Pot.

2. Secure the lid and set the vent to sealing. Manually set the cook time for 10 minutes on high pressure.

3. When cook time is up, let the pressure release naturally for 10 minutes, then manually release the remaining pressure.

4. Remove the lid, pour in the cooked pasta, and sprinkle the contents with Parmesan. Gently mix and serve.

Szechuan-Style Chicken and Broccoli

Jane Meiser, Harrisonburg, VA

Makes 4 servings
Prep. Time: 10 minutes

Needed at Time of Preparation:

1½ lb. boneless, skinless chicken thighs,
cut into 1½" cubes

2 cups broccoli florets

1 medium red bell pepper, sliced

½ cup picante sauce

2 Tbsp. light soy sauce

½ tsp. sugar

1 medium onion, chopped

2 cloves garlic, minced

½ tsp. ground ginger

2 tsp. quick-cooking tapioca

Preparation Instructions:

1. Place all ingredients in a freezer bag and smoosh around. Seal the bag, removing as much air as possible, then label it.

2. Place the freezer bag into a circular container that is slightly smaller than the diameter of your Instant Pot inner pot and freeze.

Information for Freezer Bag:

SZECHUAN-STYLE CHICKEN AND BROCCOLI

Makes 4 servings
Cook Time: 10 minutes

Needed at Time of Cooking/ Serving:

1 cup chicken stock

Cooked rice

Instructions:

1. Pour the chicken stock along with the contents of the freezer bag into the inner pot of the Instant Pot.

2. Secure the lid and set the vent to sealing. Manually set the cook time for 10 minutes on high pressure.

3. When cook time is over, let the pressure release naturally for 10 minutes, then release the remaining pressure manually.

4. Serve over the cooked rice.

Salsa Ranch Chicken with Black Beans

Hope Comerford, Clinton Township, MI

Makes 8–10 servings
Prep. Time: 10 minutes

Need at Time of Preparation:

2–3 lb. boneless, skinless chicken thighs, cut into 1½" pieces

1¼-oz. pkg. taco seasoning

1-oz. pkg. dry ranch dressing mix

1 cup salsa

10¾-oz. can cream of chicken soup

15½-oz. can black beans, drained and rinsed

Preparation Instructions:

1. Place all ingredients in a freezer bag and smoosh around until everything is well coated.

2. Seal the bag, removing as much air as possible, then label it.

3. Place the freezer bag into a circular container that is slightly smaller than the diameter of your Instant Pot inner pot and freeze.

Information for Freezer Bag:

SALSA RANCH CHICKEN WITH BLACK BEANS

Makes 8–10 servings
Cook Time: 10 minutes

Needed at Time of Cooking:

1 cup chicken stock

Serving Suggestion: This is great in tacos, on nachos, on top of a salad, on top of rice, or just on its own!

Instructions:

1. Pour the chicken stock and contents of the freezer bag into the inner pot of the Instant Pot.

2. Secure the lid and set the vent to sealing. Manually set the cook time for 10 minutes.

3. When cook time is up, let the pressure release naturally for 10 minutes, then manually release the remaining pressure.

4. Remove the chicken and shred it between two forks. Replace the chicken back in the inner pot and stir.

Easy Enchilada Shredded Chicken

Hope Comerford, Clinton Township, MI

Makes 10–14 servings
Prep. Time: 10 minutes

Needed at Time of Preparation:

5 lb. boneless, skinless chicken thighs, cut into 1½" pieces

14½-oz. can petite diced tomatoes

1 medium onion, chopped

8 oz. red enchilada sauce

½ tsp. salt

½ tsp. chili powder

½ tsp. basil

½ tsp. garlic powder

¼ tsp. pepper

Preparation Instructions:

1. Place all ingredients in a freezer bag and smoosh around until everything is mixed and coated.

2. Seal the bag, removing as much air as possible, then label it.

3. Place the freezer bag into a circular container that is slightly smaller than the diameter of your Instant Pot inner pot and freeze.

Information for Freezer Bag:

EASY ENCHILADA SHREDDED CHICKEN

Makes 10–14 servings
Cook Time: 10 minutes

Needed at Time of Cooking/ Serving:

1 cup chicken stock

Optional: Add a dollop of plain yogurt and a sprinkle of fresh cilantro.

Serving suggestion: Serve over salad, brown rice, quinoa, sweet potatoes, nachos, or soft-shell corn tortillas.

Instructions:

1. Pour the chicken stock and contents of the freezer bag into the inner pot of the Instant Pot.

2. Secure the lid and set the vent to sealing. Manually set the cook time for 10 minutes on high pressure.

3. When cook time is up, let the pressure release naturally for 10 minutes, then manually release the remaining pressure.

4. Remove the lid. Take the chicken pieces out, shred the chicken between two forks, and mix the chicken back into the juices in the pot.

5. Serve with the optional yogurt and cilantro.

Pizza in a Pot

Marianne J. Troyer, Millersburg, OH

Makes 8 servings
Prep. Time: 15 minutes

Needed at Time of Preparation:

1 lb. bulk lean sweet Italian turkey sausage, browned, drained, and cooled

28-oz. can crushed tomatoes

15½-oz. can chili beans

2¼-oz. can sliced black olives, drained

1 medium onion, chopped

1 small green bell pepper, chopped

2 cloves garlic, minced

¼ cup grated Parmesan cheese

1 Tbsp. quick-cooking tapioca

1 Tbsp. dried basil

1 bay leaf

Preparation Instructions:

1. Place all ingredients in a freezer bag.

2. Seal the bag, removing as much air as possible, then label it.

3. Place the freezer bag into a circular container that is slightly smaller than the diameter of your Instant Pot inner pot and freeze.

Information for Freezer Bag:

PIZZA IN A POT

Makes 8 servings
Cook Time: 7 minutes

Needed at Time of Cooking:

1 cup tomato juice

Serving Suggestion: Serve over pasta. Top with mozzarella cheese.

Instructions:

1. Pour the tomato juice and contents of the freezer bag into the inner pot of the Instant Pot.

2. Secure the lid and make sure the vent is set to sealing. Manually set the cook time for 7 minutes on high pressure.

3. When cook time is up, let the pressure release naturally. Discard the bay leaf.

Turkey Meat Loaf

Delores A. Gnagey, Saginaw, MI

Makes 4–5 servings
Prep. Time: 8 hours plus 15 minutes

Needed at Time of Preparation:

1 ½ lb. lean ground turkey

½ of a small onion, minced

1 ½ Tbsp. minced fresh parsley

2 egg whites

2 Tbsp. skim milk

½ tsp. dry mustard

¼ tsp. salt

⅛ tsp. ground white pepper

Pinch nutmeg

¾ cup bread crumbs

Preparation Instructions:

1. Mix together ground turkey, onion, and parsley in a medium-sized bowl. Set aside.

2. In another bowl, whisk the egg whites. Add the milk, mustard, salt, pepper, and nutmeg to the egg. Whisk to blend.

3. Add the bread crumbs to the egg mixture. Let rest 10 minutes.

4. Add the egg mixture to the meat mixture and blend well.

5. Line the inside of a 7" springform or round baking pan with 2 long sheets (8–10") of plastic wrap, perpendicular to one another. Press the meat mixture into the pan and gently seal up the plastic wrap over the top of the meat loaf.

6. Freeze 8 hours, or overnight in the pan.

7. Once frozen solid, remove the wrapped meat loaf from the pan and place in a freezer bag.

8. Seal the bag, removing as much air as possible, then label it. Place the bag in the freezer.

TURKEY MEAT LOAF

Makes 4–5 servings

Cook Time: 50 minutes ❦ *Standing Time: 10 minutes*

Needed at Time of Cooking:

1 cup water

Nonstick cooking spray

1 Tbsp. ketchup

1 Tbsp. brown sugar

Serving Suggestion: Serve alongside mashed potatoes and a vegetable or salad of your choice.

Instructions:

1. Set the trivet inside the inner pot of the Instant Pot and pour in 1 cup water.

2. Spray a 7" springform or round baking pan with nonstick cooking spray. Remove the meat loaf from the freezer bag and plastic wrap and place it into the pan.

3. Blend together ketchup and brown sugar in a small bowl. Spread mixture on top of meat. Cover the pan with aluminum foil.

4. Place the springform pan on top of the trivet inside the inner pot.

5. Secure the lid and set the vent to sealing. Manually set the cook time for 50 minutes on high pressure.

6. When cook time is up, manually release the pressure.

7. Remove the lid and use oven mitts to carefully remove the trivet from the inner pot.

8. Allow the meat loaf to stand 10 minutes before slicing to serve.

Turkey Sloppy Joes

Marla Folkerts, Holland, OH

Makes 6 servings
Prep. Time: 15 minutes

Needed at Time of Preparation:

1 ½ lb. ground turkey, browned, drained, and cooled

1 red onion, chopped

1 bell pepper, chopped

1 cup ketchup

½ teaspoons salt

1 clove garlic, minced

1 teaspoon Dijon mustard

⅛ teaspoon pepper

Preparation Instructions:

1. Place all ingredients in a freezer bag and smoosh around.

2. Seal the bag, removing as much air as possible, then label it.

3. Place the freezer bag into a circular container that is slightly smaller than the diameter of your Instant Pot inner pot and freeze.

Information for Freezer Bag:

TURKEY SLOPPY JOES

Makes 6 servings
Cook Time: 7 minutes

Needed at Time of Cooking/Serving:

1 cup chicken stock

6 (1½ oz. each) multigrain sandwich rolls

Instructions:

1. Pour the chicken stock and contents of the freezer bag into the inner pot of the Instant Pot.

2. Secure the lid and set the vent to sealing. Manually set the cook time for 7 minutes on high pressure.

3. When cook time is up, let the pressure release naturally for 5 minutes, then manually release the remaining pressure.

4. Remove the lid and set the Instant Pot to Sauté to allow the sauce to thicken.

5. Serve on sandwich rolls.

Beef Main Dishes

Easy Pot Roast and Vegetables

Tina Houk, Clinton, MO
Arlene Wines, Newton, KS

Makes 6 servings
Prep. Time: 20 minutes

Needed at Time of Preparation:

3–4-lb. chuck roast, trimmed of fat and cut into 2" chunks

4 medium carrots, cut into 2" chunks, or 1 lb. baby carrots

2 celery ribs, cut into 2" pieces

1 envelope dry onion soup mix

Preparation Instructions:

1. Place all ingredients in a freezer bag and smoosh everything around.

2. Seal the bag, removing as much air as possible, then label it.

3. Place the freezer bag into a circular container that is slightly smaller than the diameter of your Instant Pot inner pot and freeze.

Information for Freezer Bag:

EASY POT ROAST AND VEGETABLES

Makes 6 servings
Cook Time: 35 minutes

Needed at Time of Cooking:

4 medium potatoes, unpeeled, cut into 2" chunks

2 cups water

1 cup chicken stock

Instructions:

1. Place the potatoes into the inner pot. Pour the water, chicken stock, and contents of the freezer bag on top.

2. Secure the lid and make sure the vent is set to sealing. Manually set the cook time for 35 minutes on high pressure.

3. When cook time is up, let pressure release naturally.

Marinated Chuck Roast

Susan Nafziger, Canton, KS

Makes 7–8 servings
Prep. Time: 8 minutes

Needed at Time of Preparation:

1 cup olive oil

1 cup soy sauce

¼ cup red wine vinegar

½ cup chopped onions

⅛ tsp. garlic powder

¼ tsp. ground ginger

½ tsp. black pepper

½ tsp. dry mustard

3–4 lb. boneless chuck roast, cut into 2" chunks

Preparation Instructions:

1. Mix together the first 8 ingredients by whisking in a bowl, or blending in blender.

2. Place the roast in a freezer bag and pour the sauce over top.

3. Seal the bag, removing as much air as possible, then label it.

4. Place the freezer bag into a circular container that is slightly smaller than the diameter of your Instant Pot inner pot and freeze.

Information for Freezer Bag:

MARINATED CHUCK ROAST

Makes 7–8 servings
Cook Time: 20 minutes

Needed at Time of Cooking:

1 cup beef stock

Instructions:

1. Pour the beef stock and contents of the freezer bag into the inner pot of the Instant Pot.

2. Secure the lid and set the vent to sealing. Manually set the cook time for 20 minutes on high pressure.

3. When cook time is up, let the pressure release naturally.

Mexican Flavored Bottom Round Roast

David Ecker, Fair Lawn, NJ

Makes 4–6 servings
Prep. Time: 5 minutes

Needed at Time of Preparation:

2½–3 lb. bottom round roast, cut into 2" chunks

½ tsp. crushed red pepper flakes (adjust to taste)

½ tsp. chipotle pepper flakes (adjust to taste)

1 tsp. cumin

1 tsp. chili powder

1 tsp. kosher salt

15-oz. container Whole Foods Taqueria Salsa or Medium Salsa

Preparation Instructions:

1. Place all ingredients in a freezer bag and smoosh around.

2. Seal the bag, removing as much air as possible, then label it.

3. Place the freezer bag into a circular container that is slightly smaller than the diameter of your Instant Pot inner pot and freeze.

Information for Freezer Bag:

MEXICAN FLAVORED BOTTOM ROUND ROAST

Makes 4–6 servings
Cook Time: 30 minutes

Needed at Time of Cooking:

1 cup beef stock

Serving Suggestion: Shred meat and serve with 12–16 oz. tagliatelle pasta cooked separately al dente and then tossed with meat in a bowl (this will provide 8–10 servings).

Instructions:

1. Pour the stock and contents of the freezer bag into the inner pot of the Instant Pot.

2. Secure the lid and set the vent to sealing. Manually set the cook time for 30 minutes on high pressure.

3. When cook time is up, let the pressure release naturally.

Braised Beef with Cranberries

Audrey L. Kneer, Williamsfield, IL

Makes 8 servings
Prep. Time: 20 minutes

Needed at Time of Preparation:

2 lb. top round beef, cut into 2" chunks

⅛ tsp. pepper

1 tsp. salt

1 tsp. olive oil

1 turnip, peeled and chopped into 2" chunks

1 medium onion, chopped

2 cloves garlic, chopped

1 medium carrot, cut into 2" chunks

1 sprig parsley

1 bay leaf

Preparation Instructions:

1. Place all ingredients in a freezer bag and smoosh around.

2. Seal the bag, removing as much air as possible, then label it.

3. Place the freezer bag into a circular container that is slightly smaller than the diameter of your Instant Pot inner pot and freeze.

Information for Freezer Bag:

BRAISED BEEF WITH CRANBERRIES

Makes 8 servings
Cook Time: 60 minutes

Needed at Time of Cooking:

1 cup low-sugar apple juice

1 rib celery, cut into 2" chunks

1 cup fresh, or frozen (thawed), cranberries

Instructions:

1. Pour the apple juice, celery, cranberries, and contents of the freezer bag into the inner pot of the Instant Pot.

2. Secure the lid and set the vent to sealing.

3. Manually set the cook time for 60 minutes on high pressure.

4. When cook time is up, let the pressure release naturally for 10 minutes, the manually release the remaining pressure.

Beef Roast with Homemade Ginger-Orange Sauce

Beverly Hummel, Fleetwood, PA

Makes 8 servings
Prep. Time: 15 minutes

Needed at Time of Preparation:

½ tsp. salt

¼ tsp. pepper

3-lb. boneless chuck roast, cut into 2" chunks

2 cups soy sauce

½ cup brown sugar

½ cup white sugar

¼ cup minced onion

1 Tbsp. ground ginger

1 clove garlic, minced

½ cup orange juice

Preparation instructions:

1. Salt and pepper the roast on all sides and seal in a freezer bag, removing as much air as possible. Label "#1."

2. In a second freezer bag, add the remaining ingredients. Label "#2." Remove as much air as possible and seal bag.

3. Place both bags into a third freezer bag and remove as much air as possible and label with the instructions below.

4. Place the third freezer bag, meat at the bottom, into a circular container that is slightly smaller than the diameter of your Instant Pot inner pot and freeze.

BEEF ROAST WITH HOMEMADE GINGER-ORANGE SAUCE

Makes 8 servings

Cook Time: 20 minutes plus 15 minutes ☘ *Stove Cook Time: 15–20 minutes*

Needed at Time of Cooking:

1 cup water

Serving Suggestion: Serve over mashed potatoes, rice, or in sandwiches.

Instructions:

1. Place the contents of bag #2 into a bowl of hot water while you get the Instant Pot situated.

2. Place the trivet at the bottom of the inner pot of the Instant Pot and pour in the water. Place the contents of bag #1 on top of the trivet.

3. Secure the lid and set the vent to sealing. Manually set the cook time for 20 minutes on high pressure.

4. Empty the contents of bag #2 in a saucepan. Let it defrost on medium heat, then simmer for 15 minutes, stirring occasionally so it doesn't stick.

5. When the Instant Pot cook time is up, let the pressure release naturally.

6. When the pin drops, lift the cooked roast pieces into big bowl. Shred with two forks.

7. Drain drippings and broth out of inner pot.

8. Return the shredded meat to the inner pot and stir in the sauce you made on the stove from bag #2.

9. Press the Sauté function and let the meat and sauce simmer for about 15 minutes, or until heated through.

Machaca Beef

Jeanne Allen, Rye, CO

Makes 12 servings
Prep. Time: 15 minutes

Needed at Time of Preparation:

1½-lb. beef roast, cut into 2" chunks

1 large onion, sliced

4-oz. can chopped green chilies

2 beef bouillon cubes

1½ teaspoons dry mustard

½ teaspoon garlic powder

1 teaspoon seasoning salt

½ teaspoon pepper

Preparation Instructions:

1. Combine all ingredients in a freezer bag.

2. Seal the bag, removing as much air as possible, then label it.

3. Place the freezer bag into a circular container that is slightly smaller than the diameter of your Instant Pot inner pot and freeze.

Information for Freezer Bag:

MACHACA BEEF

Makes 12 servings
Cook Time: 30 minutes

Needed at Time of Cooking:

1 cup water

1 cup salsa

Serving Suggestion: Use this filling for burritos, chalupas, quesadillas, or tacos.

Instructions:

1. Pour the water and contents of the freezer bag into the inner pot of the Instant Pot.

2. Secure the lid and set the vent to sealing. Manually set the cook time for 30 minutes on high pressure.

3. When cook time is up, let the pressure release naturally.

4. Remove the beef and shred it in a bowl using two forks.

5. Combine the shredded beef, salsa, and enough of the cooking liquid from the pot to make the desired consistency.

Chuck Roast Beef Barbecue

Helen Heurich, Lititz, PA

Makes 20 servings
Prep. Time: 10 minutes

Needed at Time of Preparation:

3-lb. boneless beef chuck roast, cut into 2" chunks

⅔ cup sriracha, ketchup, or barbecue sauce

1¼ cups traditional tomato ketchup

3 Tbsp. lemon juice

2 Tbsp. Worcestershire sauce

2 Tbsp. brown sugar

1½ tsp. spicy brown prepared mustard

3 Tbsp. apple cider vinegar, *optional*

1–2 medium onions, chopped

Preparation Instructions:

1. Place all ingredients in a freezer bag and smoosh everything around.

2. Seal the bag, removing as much air as possible, then label it.

3. Place the freezer bag into a circular container that is slightly smaller than the diameter of your Instant Pot inner pot and freeze.

Information for Freezer Bag:

CHUCK ROAST BEEF BARBECUE

Makes 20 servings
Cook Time: 30 minutes

Needed at Time of Cooking/Serving:

3–4 ribs celery, cut into 2" chunks

1 cup beef broth

Sandwich rolls

Instructions:

1. Place the celery, beef broth, and contents of the freezer bag into the inner pot of the Instant Pot.

2. Secure the lid and set the vent to sealing. Manually set the cook time for 30 minutes on high pressure.

3. When cook time is up, let the pressure release naturally.

4. Remove the meat and place in a bowl. Using two forks, pull the meat apart until it's shredded. Return the shredded meat to the inner pot and mix the meat through the sauce.

5. Serve on the sandwich rolls.

Bavarian Beef

Naomi E. Fast, Hesston, KS

Makes 8 servings
Prep. Time: 15 minutes

Needed at Time of Preparation:

3-lb. boneless beef chuck roast, cut into 2" chunks

1 Tbsp. canola oil

½ cup dry red wine

3 carrots, peeled and cut into 2" chunks

3 cups sliced onions

2 large kosher dill pickles, chopped

⅓ cup German-style mustard

2 tsp. coarsely ground black pepper

2 bay leaves

¼ tsp. ground cloves

Preparation Instructions:

1. Place all ingredients in a freezer bag.

2. Seal the bag, removing as much air as possible, then label it.

3. Place the freezer bag into a circular container that is slightly smaller than the diameter of your Instant Pot inner pot and freeze.

Information for Freezer Bag:

BAVARIAN BEEF

Makes 8 servings
Cook Time: 60 minutes plus 5 minutes

Needed at Time of Cooking:

1 cup sliced celery

½ cup beef broth

½ cup water

⅓ cup flour

Serving Suggestion: Serve over noodles or spaetzle.

Instructions:

1. Place the celery, beef broth, water, and contents of the freezer bag into the inner pot of the Instant Pot.

2. Secure the lid and set the vent to sealing. Manually set the cook time to 60 minutes on high pressure.

3. When cook time is up, let the pressure release naturally.

4. Remove the meat and vegetables to large platter. Cover to keep warm.

5. Remove 1 cup of the liquid from the Instant Pot and mix with the flour. Press Sauté on the Instant Pot and add the flour/broth mixture back in, whisking. Cook until the broth is smooth and thickened.

Barbecued Brisket

Dorothy Dyer, Lee's Summit, MO

Makes 9–12 servings
Prep. Time: 10 minutes

Needed at Time of Preparation:

3–4-lb. beef brisket, cut into 2" chunks

⅓ cup Italian salad dressing

1½ tsp. liquid smoke

⅓ cup + 2 tsp. brown sugar, packed

½ tsp. celery salt

½ tsp. salt

1 Tbsp. Worcestershire sauce

½ tsp. black pepper

¼ tsp. chili powder

½ tsp. garlic powder

Preparation Instructions:

1. Place all ingredients in a freezer bag and smoosh around.

2. Seal the bag, removing as much air as possible, then label it.

3. Place the freezer bag into a circular container that is slightly smaller than the diameter of your Instant Pot inner pot and freeze.

Information for Freezer Bag:

BARBECUED BRISKET

Makes 9–12 servings
Cook Time: 45 minutes   Broil Time: 5 minutes

Needed at Time of Cooking/ Serving:

1 cup beef broth

1¼ cups barbecue sauce

Sandwich rolls

Instructions:

1. Pour the beef broth and contents of the freezer bag into the inner pot of the Instant Pot.

2. Secure the lid and set the vent to sealing. Manually set the cook time for 45 minutes on high pressure.

3. When cook time is up, let the pressure release naturally.

4. Lift the meat out of the Instant Pot and place in a baking dish.

5. Pour the barbecue sauce over the meat. Broil for 5 minutes or so, to brown. Watch carefully so it doesn't burn.

6. Serve on sandwich rolls.

Garlic Beef Stroganoff

Sharon Miller, Holmesville, OH

Makes 6 servings
Prep. Time: 30 minutes

Needed at Time of Preparation:

2 Tbsp. canola oil

1½-lb. boneless round steak, cut into thin strips, trimmed of fat

2 (4½-oz.) jars sliced mushrooms, with the juice

10¾-oz. can cream of mushroom soup

1 large onion, chopped

3 cloves garlic, minced

1 Tbsp. Worcestershire sauce

Preparation Instructions:

1. Press the Sauté button and put the oil into the Instant Pot inner pot.

2. Once the oil is heated, sauté the beef in batches, until it is lightly browned, about 2 minutes on each side. Set the beef aside on paper towels to cool and drain.

3. Once the meat has cooled, place it in a freezer bag along with the remaining ingredients.

4. Seal the bag, removing as much air as possible, then label it.

5. Place the freezer bag into a circular container that is slightly smaller than the diameter of your Instant Pot inner pot and freeze.

Information for Freezer Bag:

GARLIC BEEF STROGANOFF

Makes 6 servings
Cook Time: 8 minutes

Needed at Time of Cooking/ Serving:

½ cup beef stock

½ cup water

8-oz. brick cream cheese, room temperature, cut into 1" chunks

6 servings cooked egg noodles

Instructions:

1. Pour the beef stock, water and contents of the freezer bag into the inner pot of the Instant Pot.

2. Secure the lid and set the vent to sealing. Manually set the cook time for 8 minutes on high pressure.

3. When cook time is up, let the pressure release naturally for 10 minutes, then manually release the remaining pressure.

4. Remove the lid, then set the Instant Pot to the Sauté function. Stir in cream cheese chunks until smooth.

5. Serve over the egg noodles.

Beef Burgundy with Mushrooms

Rosemarie Fitzgerald, Gibsonia, PA

Makes 6 servings
Prep. Time: 10 minutes

Needed at Time of Preparation:

2–3-lb. boneless chuck roast, cut into
1½" pieces

1 cup onions, chopped

2 cloves garlic

¼–½ tsp. marjoram

½ lb. fresh mushrooms, sliced

Preparation Instructions:

1. Place all ingredients in a freezer bag.

2. Seal the bag, removing as much air as possible, then label it.

3. Place the freezer bag into a circular container that is slightly smaller than the diameter of your Instant Pot inner pot and freeze.

Information for Freezer Bag:

BEEF BURGUNDY WITH MUSHROOMS

Makes 6 servings
Cook Time: 30 minutes plus 10–15 minutes

Needed at Time of Cooking:

½ cup burgundy wine

½ cup water

6-oz. can tomato paste

Dash sugar

Serving Suggestion: Serve over cooked noodles, rice, or with potatoes.

Instructions:

1. Pour the burgundy wine and water into the inner pot of the Instant Pot along with the contents of the freezer bag.

2. Secure the lid and set the vent to sealing. Manually set the cook time for 30 minutes on high pressure.

3. When cook time is up, let the pressure release naturally.

4. Switch the Instant Pot to the Sauté function. Stir in the tomato paste and sugar. Cook another 10–15 minutes, uncovered, to allow sauce to thicken.

Steak Stroganoff

Hope Comerford, Clinton Twp, MI

Makes 6 servings
Prep. Time: 30 minutes

Needed at Time of Preparation:

3–4 Tbsp. olive oil

½ cup flour

½ tsp. garlic powder

½ tsp. onion powder

½ tsp. salt

⅛ tsp. pepper

2-lb. boneless beef chuck roast, trimmed of fat, cut into 1½" × ½" strips.

10¾-oz. can condensed cream of mushroom soup

⅓ cup Liquid Aminos or soy sauce

9-oz. sliced mushrooms

½ cup chopped red onion

Preparation Instructions:

1. Place the oil in the Instant Pot and press Sauté.

2. Combine flour, garlic powder, onion powder, salt, and pepper in a medium bowl. Stir the beef pieces through the flour mixture until they are evenly coated.

3. Lightly brown the steak pieces in the oil in the Instant Pot, about 2 minutes each side. Let them drain and cool on a paper towel. Do this in batches, adding more oil to the pot with each batch if needed. Set them aside to cool.

4. Once the steak pieces are cool, place the steak pieces and remaining ingredients into a gallon-sized freezer bag.

5. Seal the bag, removing as much air as possible, then label it.

6. Place the freezer bag into a circular container that is slightly smaller than the diameter of your Instant Pot inner pot and freeze.

STEAK STROGANOFF

Makes 6 servings

Cook Time: 10 minutes plus 5 minutes

Needed at Time of Cooking/ Serving:

1 cup beef stock

½ cup fat-free sour cream

6 servings cooked egg noodles or brown rice ramen

Instructions:

1. Pour the stock and contents of the freezer bag into the inner pot of the Instant Pot.

2. Secure the lid and set the vent to sealing. Manually set the cook time for 10 minutes on high pressure.

3. When cook time is up, let the pressure release naturally for 10 minutes, then release the rest manually.

4. Remove the lid and switch the Instant Pot to the Sauté function. Stir in the sour cream. Let the sauce come to a boil and cook for about 5 minutes.

5. Serve over the cooked egg noodles or brown rice ramen.

Hungarian Beef with Paprika

Maureen Csikasz, Wakefield, MA

Makes 9 servings
Prep. Time: 15 minutes

Needed at Time of Preparation:

3-lb. boneless chuck roast, cut into
2" chunks

2–3 medium onions, coarsely chopped

5 Tbsp. sweet paprika

¾ tsp. salt

¼ tsp. black pepper

½ tsp. caraway seeds

1 clove garlic, chopped

½ green bell pepper, sliced

Preparation Instructions:

1. Place all ingredients in a freezer bag and smoosh around.

2. Seal the bag, removing as much air as possible, then label it.

3. Place the freezer bag into a circular container that is slightly smaller than the diameter of your Instant Pot inner pot and freeze.

Information for Freezer Bag:

HUNGARIAN BEEF WITH PAPRIKA

Makes 9 servings
Cook Time: 30 minutes

Needed at Time of Cooking/ Serving:

½ cup water

½ cup beef stock

½ cup sour cream, *optional*

Fresh parsley

Serving Suggestion: Serve with buttered noodles or potatoes.

Instructions:

1. Pour the water, beef stock, and contents of the freezer bag into the inner pot of the Instant Pot.

4. Secure the lid and set the vent to sealing. Manually set the cook time for 30 minutes.

3. When cook time is up, let the pressure release naturally.

4. When serving, dollop with the sour cream, if desired. Garnish with fresh parsley.

Three-Pepper Steak

Renee Hankins, Narvon, PA

Makes 10 servings
Prep. Time: 15 minutes

Needed at Time of Preparation:

3-lb. beef flank steak, cut in ½" x 2" slices

3 bell peppers—one red, one orange, and one yellow pepper (or any combination of colors), cut into ¼"-thick slices

2 cloves garlic, sliced

1 large onion, sliced

1 teaspoon ground cumin

½ teaspoon dried oregano

1 bay leaf

Salt to taste

14½-oz. can diced tomatoes in juice

Jalapeño slices, *optional*

Preparation Instructions:

1. Place all ingredients in a freezer bag.

2. Seal the bag, removing as much air as possible, then label it.

3. Place the freezer bag into a circular container that is slightly smaller than the diameter of your Instant Pot inner pot and freeze.

Information for Freezer Bag:

THREE-PEPPER STEAK

Makes 10 servings
Cook Time: 10 minutes

Needed at Time of Cooking:

½ cup water

½ cup beef stock

Serving Suggestion: Serve over noodles, rice, or torn tortillas.

Instructions:

1. Pour the water, beef stock, and contents of the freezer bag into the inner pot of the Instant Pot.

2. Secure the lid and make sure vent is set to sealing. Manually set the cook time for 10 minutes on high pressure.

3. When cook time is up, let the pressure release naturally for 10 minutes, then manually release the remaining pressure.

Beef Broccoli

Anita Troyer, Fairview, MI

Makes 6 servings
Prep. Time: 15 minutes

Needed at Time of Preparation:

2-lb. beef flank steak, cut in
½" x 2" slices

½ cup diced onion

3 cloves garlic, minced

¾ cup beef broth

½ cup soy sauce

¼ cup brown sugar

2 Tbsp. sesame oil

¼ tsp. red pepper flakes

¼ tsp. black pepper

Preparation Instructions:

1. Place all ingredients in a freezer bag and smoosh around.

2. Seal the bag, removing as much air as possible, then label it.

3. Place the freezer bag into a circular container that is slightly smaller than the diameter of your Instant Pot inner pot and freeze.

Information for Freezer Bag:

BEEF BROCCOLI

Makes 6 servings
Cook Time: 10 minutes plus 5–8 minutes

Needed at Time of Cooking:

½ cup water

½ cup beef stock

1 lb. broccoli, chopped

3 Tbsp. water

3 Tbsp. cornstarch

Serving suggestion: Serve over rice.

Instructions:

1. Pour the water, beef stock, and contents of the freezer bag into the inner pot of the Instant Pot.

2. Secure the lid and set the vent to sealing. Manually set the cook time for 10 minutes on high pressure.

3. When cook time is up, let the pressure release naturally for 10 minutes, then manually release the remaining pressure.

4. Switch the Instant Pot to the Sauté function. Add the broccoli to the inner pot and stir.

5. In a small bowl, stir together the water and cornstarch. Add to the pot and stir until the mixture thickens, 5–8 minutes.

Marinated Flank Steak with Broccoli

Amanda Gross, Souderton, PA

Makes 6 servings
Prep. Time: 10 minutes

Needed at Time of Preparation:

2 lb. flank steak, cut in ½" x 2" slices

½ cup soy sauce

¼ cup brown sugar

2 cloves garlic, minced

I Tbsp. sesame oil

Preparation Instructions:

1. Place all ingredients in a freezer bag and massage to combine all ingredients.

2. Seal the bag, removing as much air as possible, then label it.

3. Place the freezer bag into a circular container that is slightly smaller than the diameter of your Instant Pot inner pot and freeze.

Information for Freezer Bag:

MARINATED FLANK STEAK WITH BROCCOLI

Makes 4–6 servings
Cook Time: 10 minutes plus 5 minutes

Needed at Time of Cooking/ Serving:

1 cup beef broth

2 cups broccoli florets, chopped

Cooked rice

Instructions:

1. Place the beef broth and contents of the freezer bag into the inner pot of the Instant Pot.

2. Secure the lid and set the vent to sealing. Manually set the cook time for 10 minutes on high pressure.

3. When cook time is up, let the pressure release naturally for 10 minutes, then manually release the remaining pressure.

4. Remove the lid. Switch the pot to the Sauté function. Stir in the the broccoli. Let it cook for about 5 minutes, stirring frequently, or until desired doneness.

5. Serve over the cooked rice.

Philly Cheese Steaks

Michele Ruvola, Vestal, NY

Makes 6 servings
Prep. Time: 10 minutes

Needed at Time of Preparation:

2½ lb. flank steak, cut in ½" x 2" slices

1 red pepper, sliced

1 green pepper, sliced

1 onion, sliced

2 cloves garlic, minced

1 tsp. salt

½ tsp. black pepper

0.7-oz. pkg. dry Italian dressing mix

Preparation Instructions:

1. Place all ingredients in a freezer bag.

2. Seal the bag, removing as much air as possible, then label it.

3. Place the freezer bag into a circular container that is slightly smaller than the diameter of your Instant Pot inner pot and freeze.

Information for Freezer Bag:

PHILLY CHEESE STEAKS

Makes 6 servings
Cook Time: 10 minutes ❦ Broil Time: 5 minutes

Needed at Time of Cooking/ Serving:

1½ cups beef stock

6 hoagie rolls

6 slices of provolone cheese

Instructions:

1. Pour the beef stock and contents of the freezer bag into the inner pot of the Instant Pot.

2. Secure the lid and set the vent to sealing. Manually set the cook time for 10 minutes on high pressure.

3. When cook time is up, let the pressure release naturally for 10 minutes, then manually release the remaining pressure.

4. Scoop meat and vegetables onto the hoagie rolls.

5. Top with provolone cheese and put on a baking sheet.

6. Broil in oven for 5 minutes.

7. Pour remaining juice from the pot into cups for dipping.

Italian Cheesesteak Sandwiches

Jennifer Archer, Kalona, IA

Makes 8–10 servings
Prep. Time: 10 minutes

Needed at Time of Preparation:

3-lb. boneless beef chuck roast, cut into
2" chunks

1 envelope dry Italian dressing mix

2–3 bay leaves

1 Tbsp. dried basil

1 Tbsp. dried oregano

2–3 tsp. garlic powder, according to taste

¼–½ tsp. coarsely ground black pepper,
according to taste

Preparation Instructions:

1. Place all ingredients in a freezer bag and smoosh together.

2. Seal the bag, removing as much air as possible, then label it.

3. Place the freezer bag into a circular container that is slightly smaller than the diameter of your Instant Pot inner pot and freeze.

Information for Freezer Bag:

ITALIAN CHEESESTEAK SANDWICHES

Makes 8–10 servings
Cook Time: 30 minutes   Broil Time: 2–3 minutes

Needed at Time of Cooking/ Serving:

1 cup beef broth

8 or 10 steak rolls

8 or 10 provolone or mozzarella cheese slices

Instructions:

1. Pour the beef broth and contents of the freezer bag into the inner pot of the Instant Pot.

2. Secure the lid and set the vent to sealing. Manually set the cook time for 30 minutes on high pressure.

3. When cook time is done, let the pressure release naturally.

4. Lift the roast chunks out of the Instant Pot and into a bowl, and use two forks to shred the meat. Fish out bay leaves and discard.

5. Return the shredded meat to the inner pot and stir through the sauce.

6. Place rolls open-faced on baking sheet. Using a slotted spoon, pile each roll with beef and slice of cheese. Place under broiler for 2–3 minutes, until cheese is bubbly.

Italian Beef Sandwiches

Hope Comerford, Clinton Township, MI

Makes 6–8 servings
Prep. Time: 5 minutes

Needed at Time of Preparation:

3½–4½-lb. English roast, cut into 2" chunks

16-oz. jar mild pepper rings, juice included

Preparation Instructions:

1. Place all ingredients in a freezer bag.

2. Seal the bag, removing as much air as possible, then label it.

3. Place the freezer bag into a circular container that is slightly smaller than the diameter of your Instant Pot inner pot and freeze.

Information for Freezer Bag:

ITALIAN BEEF SANDWICHES

Makes 6–8 servings
Cook Time: 30 minutes   ❧   Oven Time: 8 minutes

Needed at Time of Cooking/ Serving:

1 cup beef stock

6–8 sub buns

Nonstick cooking spray

Butter

6–8 large slices provolone or mozzarella cheese

Instructions:

1. Pour the beef stock and the contents of the freezer bag into the inner pot of the Instant Pot.

2. Secure the lid and set the vent to sealing. Manually set the cook time for 30 minutes on high pressure.

3. When cook time is up, let the pressure release naturally.

4. Preheat the oven to 400°F.

5. Remove the meat and shred with two forks. Place it back in the inner pot and stir with the juices.

6. Place each sub bun open-faced on a foil-lined, cookie sheet sprayed with nonstick cooking spray. Spread a bit of butter on each side. Place the cheese on top of each bun. Place them in the oven for about 8 minutes, or until the bread is slightly toasted and the cheese is melted.

7. Remove the sub buns from the oven and place a good portion of Italian beef on top. Enjoy!

Instant Pot Boneless Short Ribs

Hope Comerford, Clinton Township, MI

Makes 4 servings
Prep. Time: 10 minutes

Needed at Time of Preparation:

3 lb. boneless short ribs, cut into 2" chunks

½ tsp. salt

⅛ tsp. pepper

1 large onion, sliced

6 cloves garlic, smashed

¼ cup balsamic vinegar

¾ cup red wine

4 carrots, cut into 2" chunks

1 sprig rosemary

1 sprig thyme

Preparation Instructions:

1. Place all ingredients in a freezer bag and smoosh it around.

2. Seal the bag, removing as much air as possible, then label it.

3. Place the freezer bag into a circular container that is slightly smaller than the diameter of your Instant Pot inner pot and freeze.

Information for Freezer Bag:

INSTANT POT BONELESS SHORT RIBS

Makes 4 servings
Cook Time: 50 minutes plus 3–5 minutes

Needed at Time of Cooking:

1 cup beef stock

2 Tbsp. cold water

2 Tbsp. cornstarch

Serving suggestion: Serve with mashed or baked potatoes.

Instructions:

1. Pour the beef stock and contents of the freezer bag into the inner pot of the Instant Pot.

2. Secure the lid and set the vent to sealing. Manually set the cook time for 50 minutes on high pressure.

3. When cook time is up, let the pressure release naturally for 20 minutes, then manually release the remaining pressure.

4. Switch the Instant Pot to the Sauté function.

5. Mix the cold water and cornstarch. Gently stir this mixture into the contents of the inner pot and let simmer until the sauce is thickened a bit, about 3–5 minutes.

6. Serve the short ribs and carrots with the sauce spooned over the top.

Fabulous Fajitas

Phyllis Good, Lancaster, PA

Makes 4 servings
Prep. Time: 15 minutes

Needed at Time of Preparation:

1–1½-lb. flank steak, cut in
½" x 2" slices

1 green bell pepper, cut in strips

1 yellow onion, sliced

2 Tbsp. lemon juice

1 clove garlic, minced

1½ tsp. cumin

½ tsp. red pepper flakes

1 tsp. seasoning salt

2 Tbsp. Worcestershire sauce

1 tsp. chili powder

Preparation Instructions:

1. Place all ingredients in a freezer bag and smoosh around to coat everything evenly.

2. Seal the bag, removing as much air as possible, then label it.

3. Place the freezer bag into a circular container that is slightly smaller than the diameter of your Instant Pot inner pot and freeze.

Information for Freezer Bag:

FABULOUS FAJITAS

Makes 4 servings
Cook Time: 10 minutes

Needed at Time of Cooking/ Serving:

1 cup beef stock

6–8 warmed tortillas

Optional sour cream, chopped fresh cilantro, salsa, shredded cheese, etc.

Instructions:

1. Pour the stock and contents of the freezer bag into the inner pot of the Instant Pot.

2. Secure the lid and set the vent to sealing. Manually set the cook time for 10 minutes on high pressure.

3. When cook time is up, let the pressure release naturally for 10 minutes, then release the remaining pressure manually.

4. Spoon mixture into warm tortillas. Top with the optional toppings.

Saucy Tacos

Sarah Herr, Goshen, IN

Makes 8 servings
Prep. Time: 10 minutes

Needed at Time of Preparation:

2-lb. flank steak, cut in ½" x 2" slices

1 green bell pepper, chopped

1 onion, chopped

1 cup salsa

2 Tbsp., or 1 envelope, taco seasoning

Preparation Instructions:

1. Place all ingredients in a freezer bag and smoosh around to coat everything.

2. Seal the bag, removing as much air as possible, then label it.

3. Place the freezer bag into a circular container that is slightly smaller than the diameter of your Instant Pot inner pot and freeze.

Information for Freezer Bag:

SAUCY TACOS

Makes 8 servings
Cook Time: 30 minutes

Needed at Time of Cooking/ Serving:

1 cup water

Tortillas or taco shells

Instructions:

1. Pour the water and contents of the freezer bag into the inner pot of the Instant Pot.

2. Secure the lid and make sure the vent is set to sealing. Manually set the cook time for 30 minutes on high pressure.

3. When cook time is up, allow the pressure to release naturally for 10 minutes, then manually release the remaining pressure.

4. Shred the meat with two forks, then mix with the contents of the Instant Pot.

5. Serve in the tortillas or taco shells.

Meat Loaf

Colleen Heatwole, Burton, MI

Makes 6–8 servings
Prep. Time: 10 minutes

Needed at Time of Preparation:

2 lb. ground beef

2 eggs

⅔ cup dry quick oats

½ envelope of dry onion soup mix

½–1 tsp. liquid smoke

1 tsp. ground mustard

¼ cup ketchup

Preparation instructions:

1. In a bowl, mix all of the ingredients.

2. Line the inside of a 7" springform or round baking pan with two long sheets (8–10") of plastic wrap, perpendicular to one another. Press the meat mixture into the pan and gently seal up the plastic wrap over the top of the meat loaf.

3. Freeze overnight in the pan.

4. Once frozen solid, remove the wrapped meat loaf from the pan and place in a freezer bag. Seal the bag, removing as much air as possible, then label it. Place the bag in the freezer.

MEAT LOAF

Makes 6–8 servings

Cook Time: 50 minutes   ❧   Stand Time: 10 minutes

Needed at Time of Cooking:

1 cup water

Nonstick cooking spray

2 Tbsp. ketchup

2 Tbsp. brown sugar

Serving Suggestion: Serve alongside mashed potatoes and a vegetable or salad of your choice.

Instructions:

1. Set the trivet inside the inner pot of the Instant Pot and pour in 1 cup water.

2. Spray a 7" springform or round baking pan with nonstick cooking spray. Remove the meat loaf from the freezer bag and plastic wrap and place it into the pan.

3. Blend together ketchup and brown sugar in a small bowl. Spread mixture on top of meat. Cover the pan with aluminum foil.

4. Place the springform pan on top of the trivet inside the inner pot. Secure the lid and set the vent to sealing.

5. Manually set the cook time for 50 minutes on high pressure.

6. When cook time is up, manually release the pressure.

7. Remove the lid and use oven mitts to carefully remove the trivet from the inner pot.

8. Allow the meat loaf to stand 10 minutes before slicing to serve.

Guinness Corned Beef

Bob Coffey, New Windsor, NY

Makes 10 servings
Prep. Time: 5 minutes

Needed at Time of Preparation:

3–4-lb. corned beef with seasoning
packet, cut into 2–3 pieces

14.9-oz. can Guinness stout

1 bay leaf

¼ tsp. mustard seeds

¼ tsp. caraway seeds

¼ tsp. peppercorns

Preparation Instructions:

1. Place all ingredients in a freezer bag.

2. Seal the bag, removing as much air as possible, then label it. *Be sure to label the exact weight of your corned beef so you remember for later. You will need this information for cook time.*

3. Place the freezer bag into a circular container that is slightly smaller than the diameter of your Instant Pot inner pot. You want the meat to be spread out and overlapping as little as possible. Freeze.

(Continued on next page)

GUINNESS CORNED BEEF

Makes 10 servings

Cook Time: 102–136 minutes plus 3 minutes

Needed at Time of Cooking:

1 cup water

4 cups chopped cabbage

1 large onion, chopped

1-lb. bag baby carrots

Serving suggestion: Serve with mashed potatoes and coarse mustard or horseradish.

Instructions:

1. Place the trivet into the bottom of the inner pot and pour in the water.

2. Place the contents of the freezer bag onto the trivet.

3. Secure the lid and set the vent to sealing. Manually set the cook time for 34 minutes per pound of corned beef. If you have a 3-lb. corned beef, your cook time will be 102 minutes. If you have a 4-lb. corned beef, you will set the cook time for 136 minutes.

4. When cook time is up, let the pressure release naturally for 15 minutes, then manually release the remaining pressure. Remove the corned beef and cover.

5. Place the vegetables into the inner pot.

6. Secure the lid and set the vent to sealing. Manually set the cook time for 3 minutes on high pressure.

7. When cook time is up, manually release the pressure.

8. Discard the bay leaf. Serve the meat and vegetables.

Beef Goulash

Colleen Heatwole, Burton, MI

Makes 6 servings
Prep. Time: 15 minutes

Needed at Time of Preparation:

2 lb. beef stew meat, cut into 2" pieces

1 large onion, chopped

3 carrots, cut into 2" chunks

1 medium red bell pepper chopped, sliced

¼ cup ketchup

2 tsp. Worcestershire sauce

2 tsp. paprika

2 tsp. minced garlic

1 tsp. salt

Preparation Instructions:

1. Place all ingredients in a freezer bag and smoosh around.

2. Seal the bag, removing as much air as possible, then label it.

3. Place the freezer bag into a circular container that is slightly smaller than the diameter of your Instant Pot inner pot and freeze.

Information for Freezer Bag:

BEEF GOULASH

Makes 6 servings
Cook Time: 50 minutes

Needed at Time of Cooking:

1 cup beef broth

Serving Suggestion: Mashed potatoes and green beans go well as sides.

Instructions:

1. Pour the broth and contents of the freezer bag into the inner pot of the Instant Pot.

2. Secure the lid and set the vent to sealing. Manually set the cook time for 50 minutes on high pressure.

3. When cook time is up, let the pressure release naturally for 20 minutes, then manually release the remaining pressure.

Pork Main Dishes

Garlic Pork Roast

Earnie Zimmerman, Mechanicsburg, PA

Makes 10 servings
Prep. Time: 15–20 minutes

Needed at Time of Preparation:

3-lb. boneless pork loin roast, cut into 1" cubes

1 tsp. salt

½ tsp. coarsely ground black pepper

1 medium onion, sliced

6 cloves garlic, peeled

8 strips (each 3" x ½") fresh lemon peel

1 lb. baby carrots

½ tsp. dried thyme

Preparation Instructions:

1. Place all ingredients in a freezer bag and smoosh around.

2. Seal the bag, removing as much air as possible, then label it.

3. Place the freezer bag into a circular container that is slightly smaller than the diameter of your Instant Pot inner pot and freeze.

Information for Freezer Bag:

GARLIC PORK ROAST

Makes 10 servings
Cook Time: 20 minutes

Needed at Time of Cooking:

1 cup chicken broth

1½ lb. red potatoes, cut in ½"-thick slices

Serving Suggestion: Serve with rice or couscous and a salad.

Instructions:

1. Pour the chicken broth into the inner pot of the Instant Pot. Add in the potatoes and contents of the freezer bag.

2. Secure the lid and set the vent to sealing. Manually set the cook time for 20 minutes on high pressure.

3. When cook time is up, let the pressure release naturally for 10 minutes, then manually release the remaining pressure.

Honey-Orange Pork Roast

Earnie Zimmerman, Mechanicsburg, PA

Makes 8–10 servings
Prep. Time: 5 minutes

Needed at Time of Preparation:

4-lb. boneless pork butt roast

1 tsp. salt

⅛ tsp. pepper

¼–½ cup honey

1 cup fresh or frozen cranberries

Preparation Instructions:

1. Place all ingredients in a freezer bag and smoosh around to coat roast well.

2. Seal the bag, removing as much air as possible, then label it.

3. Place the freezer bag into a circular container that is slightly smaller than the diameter of your Instant Pot inner pot and freeze.

Information for Freezer Bag:

HONEY-ORANGE PORK ROAST

Makes 8–10 servings
Cook Time: 15 minutes

Needed at Time of Cooking:

1 cup orange juice

4–5 good-sized sweet potatoes, peeled and cut into 1" cubes

2 good-sized tart apples, cored and quartered

Instructions:

1. Pour the orange juice, contents of the freezer bag, sweet potato chunks, and apple quarters into the inner pot of the Instant Pot.

2. Secure the lid and set the vent to sealing. Manually set the cook time for 15 minutes on high pressure.

3. When cook time is up, let the pressure release naturally for 20 minutes, then manually release any remaining pressure.

4. Place the chunks of meat, sweet potatoes, and apples, along with broth, in a deep platter or bowl to serve.

Brown Sugar and Dijon-Marinated Pork Roast

J. B. Miller, Indianapolis, IN

Makes 4–6 servings
Prep. Time: 10 minutes

Needed at Time of Preparation:

2-lb. pork loin roast, cut into 1" cubes

½ cup soy sauce

¼ cup sherry vinegar

½ tsp. Dijon mustard

¼ cup brown sugar

Preparation Instructions:

1. Place all ingredients in a freezer bag and smoosh around.

2. Seal the bag, removing as much air as possible, then label it.

3. Place the freezer bag into a circular container that is slightly smaller than the diameter of your Instant Pot inner pot and freeze.

Information for Freezer Bag:

BROWN SUGAR AND DIJON-MARINATED PORK ROAST

Makes 4–6 servings
Cook Time: 20 minutes

Needed at Time of Cooking:

1 cup chicken stock

Instructions:

1. Pour the chicken stock and contents of the freezer bag into the inner pot of the Instant Pot.

2. Secure the lid and set the vent to sealing. Manually set the cook time for 20 minutes on high pressure.

3. When cook time is up, let the pressure release naturally for 10 minutes, then manually release any remaining pressure.

Easy Pork Loin

Colleen Heatwole, Burton, MI

Makes 4–5 servings
Prep. Time: 5 minutes

Needed at Time of Preparation:

1½-lb. pork loin, cut into 1" cubes

2 Tbsp. soy sauce

2 Tbsp. tamari sauce

¼ tsp. ground ginger

½ tsp. garlic powder

Preparation Instructions:

1. Place all ingredients in a freezer bag and smoosh around.

2. Seal the bag, removing as much air as possible, then label it.

3. Place the freezer bag into a circular container that is slightly smaller than the diameter of your Instant Pot inner pot and freeze.

Information for Freezer Bag:

EASY PORK LOIN

Makes 4–5 servings
Cook Time: 20 minutes

Needed at Time of Cooking:

1 cup chicken stock or white wine

Serving Suggestion: Goes well with sweet potatoes.

Instructions:

1. Pour the stock or wine into the inner pot of the Instant Pot along with the contents of the freezer bag.

2. Secure the lid and set the vent to sealing. Manually set the cook time for 20 minutes on high pressure.

3. When cook time is up, let the pressure release naturally for 10 minutes, then manually release any remaining pressure.

4. If desired, meat may be shredded before serving.

Salsa Verde Pork

Hope Comerford, Clinton Township, MI

Makes 6 servings
Prep. Time: 20 minutes

Needed at Time of Preparation:

1½ lb. boneless pork loin, cut into 1" cubes

1 large sweet onion, halved and sliced

14-oz. can diced tomatoes

16-oz. jar salsa verde (green salsa)

4 cloves garlic, minced

1 tsp. cumin

½ tsp. chili powder

Preparation Instructions:

1. Place all ingredients in a freezer bag and smoosh around.

2. Seal the bag, removing as much air as possible, then label it.

3. Place the freezer bag into a circular container that is slightly smaller than the diameter of your Instant Pot inner pot and freeze.

Information for Freezer Bag:

SALSA VERDE PORK

Makes 6 servings
Cook Time: 20 minutes

Needed at Time of Cooking:

½ cup chicken stock

½ cup dry white wine

Serving suggestion: Serve over cooked brown rice or quinoa.

Instructions:

1. Pour the stock, wine, and contents of the freezer bag into the inner pot of the Instant Pot.

2. Secure the lid and set the vent to sealing. Manually set the cook time for 20 minutes on high pressure.

3. When cook time is up, let the pressure release naturally for 10 minutes, then manually release any remaining pressure.

4. Break apart the pork with two forks and mix with contents of the inner pot.

Philippine Ulam

Carol Eveleth, Cheyenne, WY

Makes 4–6 servings
Prep. Time: 10 minutes

Needed at Time of Preparation:

2 lb. pork loin or shoulder, cut into
1" chunks

¼ tsp. black pepper

3 bell peppers, diced

¼ cup lemon juice

½ cup soy sauce

Preparation Instructions:

1. Place all ingredients in a freezer bag and smoosh around.

2. Seal the bag, removing as much air as possible, then label it.

3. Place the freezer bag into a circular container that is slightly smaller than the diameter of your Instant Pot inner pot and freeze.

Information for Freezer Bag:

PHILIPPINE ULAM

Makes 4–6 servings
Cook Time: 20 minutes

Needed at Time of Cooking:

2 cups water

4–5 cups cubed potatoes

Serving suggestion: Serve over cooked rice.

Instructions:

1. Place the water, potatoes, and contents of the freezer bag into the inner pot of the Instant Pot.

2. Secure the lid and set the vent to sealing. Manually set the cook time for 20 minutes on high pressure.

3. When cook time is up, allow the pressure to release naturally for 10 minutes, then manually release any remaining pressure.

Carnitas

Hope Comerford, Clinton Township, MI

Makes 12 servings
Prep. Time: 10 minutes

Needed at Time of Preparation:

2 lb. pork shoulder roast, cut into 1" chunks

1 ½ tsp. kosher salt

½ tsp. pepper

2 tsp. cumin

5 cloves garlic, minced

1 tsp. oregano

3 bay leaves

Preparation Instructions:

1. Place all ingredients in a freezer bag and smoosh around to coat roast well.

2. Seal the bag, removing as much air as possible, then label it.

3. Place the freezer bag into a circular container that is slightly smaller than the diameter of your Instant Pot inner pot and freeze.

Information for Freezer Bag:

CARNITAS

Makes 12 servings
Cook Time: 15 minutes

Needed at Time of Cooking/ Serving:

2 cups chicken stock

2 Tbsp. lime juice

1 tsp. lime zest

12 6" gluten-free white corn tortillas, warmed

Instructions:

1. Pour the chicken stock and contents of the freezer bag into the inner pot of the Instant Pot.

2. Secure the lid and set the vent to sealing. Manually set the cook time for 15 minutes on high pressure.

3. When cook time is up, let the pressure release naturally.

4. Add the lime juice and lime zest to the inner pot and stir. You may choose to shred the pork if you wish.

5. Serve on the white corn tortillas.

Ginger Pork Chops

Mary Fisher, Leola, PA

Makes 4 servings
Prep. Time: 5 minutes

Needed at Time of Preparation:

4–5 thick-cut boneless pork chops
(1–1½" thick)

⅛ tsp. pepper

2 cloves garlic, minced

⅓ cup low-sodium soy sauce or tamari

⅓ cup honey

Dash ground ginger

Preparation Instructions:

1. Place all ingredients in a freezer bag and smoosh around.

2. Seal the bag, removing as much air as possible, then label it.

3. Place the freezer bag into a circular container that is slightly smaller than the diameter of your Instant Pot inner pot, spreading out the pork chops so they are overlapping as little as possible, and freeze.

Information for Freezer Bag:

GINGER PORK CHOPS

Makes 4 servings
Cook Time: 12 minutes plus 5 minutes

Needed at Time of Cooking/Serving:

1 cup chicken stock

1 Tbsp. cornstarch

1 Tbsp. cold water

2 Tbsp. sliced green onion

Instructions:

1. Place the trivet into the inner pot of the Instant Pot and pour in the chicken stock. Empty the contents of the freezer bag on top of the trivet.

2. Secure the lid and set the vent to sealing. Manually set the cook time for 12 minutes on high pressure.

3. When cook time is up, let the pressure release naturally.

4. Remove the pork chops. Set them aside on a clean plate or serving platter.

5. Mix together the cornstarch and water. Set the Instant Pot to Sauté and whisk the cornstarch mixture into the sauce in the inner pot. Let the sauce thicken to your liking, stirring often, or about 5 minutes

6. When you are ready to serve, pour some of the sauce over each pork chop and sprinkle with green onion.

Raspberry Balsamic Pork Chops

Hope Comerford, Clinton Township, MI

Makes 4–6 servings
Prep. Time: 5 minutes

Needed at Time of Preparation:

4–5 lb. thick-cut pork chops

¼ cup raspberry balsamic vinegar

2 Tbsp. olive oil

½ tsp. kosher salt

½ tsp. garlic powder

¼ tsp. basil

Preparation Instructions:

1. Place all ingredients in a freezer bag and smoosh around.

2. Seal the bag, removing as much air as possible, then label it.

3. Place the freezer bag into a circular container that is slightly smaller than the diameter of your Instant Pot inner pot, spreading out the pork chops so they are overlapping as little as possible, and freeze.

Information for Freezer Bag:

RASPBERRY BALSAMIC PORK CHOPS

Makes 4–6 servings
Cook Time: 12 minutes

Needed at Time of Cooking:

½ cup water

Serving Suggestion: Goes well with a salad and baked sweet potatoes.

Instructions:

1. Place the trivet into the inner pot of the Instant Pot and pour in the water. Empty the contents of the freezer bag on top of the trivet.

2. Secure the lid and set the vent to sealing. Manually set the cook time for 12 minutes on high pressure.

3. When cook time is up, let the pressure release naturally.

Tender Tasty Ribs

Carol Eveleth, Cheyenne, WY

Makes 2–3 servings
Prep. Time: 10 minutes

Needed at Time of Preparation:

2 tsp. salt

2 tsp. black pepper

1 tsp. garlic powder

1 tsp. onion powder

1 slab baby back ribs, membranes removed, cut into 3 pieces

Preparation Instructions:

1. Mix salt, pepper, garlic powder, and onion powder together. Rub seasoning mixture on both sides of the rib slab pieces. Place the pieces in a freezer bag.

2. Seal the bag, removing as much air as possible, then label it.

3. Place the freezer bag into a circular container that is slightly smaller than the diameter of your Instant Pot inner pot and freeze.

TENDER TASTY RIBS

Makes 2–3 servings

Cook Time: 32 minutes ❧ *Broil Time: 5–10 minutes*

Needed at Time of Cooking:

1 cup water

1 cup barbecue sauce, *divided*

Instructions:

1. Place the trivet into the inner pot of the Instant Pot and pour in the water. Place the ribs onto the trivet and drizzle with ¼ cup of the barbecue sauce.

2. Secure the lid and set the vent to sealing. Manually set the cook time for 32 minutes on high pressure.

3. When cook time is up, let the pressure release naturally for 5 minutes, then manually release the remaining pressure.

4. Turn the oven on to broil (or heat your grill) while you're waiting for the 5-minute resting time.

5. Remove the ribs from the Instant Pot and place them on a baking sheet. Slather both sides with the remaining ¾ cup sauce.

6. Place the ribs under the broiler (or on grill) for 5 to 10 minutes, watching carefully so they don't burn. Remove and brush with a bit more sauce if desired. Pull apart and dig in!

Jiffy Jambalaya

Carole M. Mackie, Williamsfield, IL

Makes 6 servings
Prep. Time: 8 minutes

Needed at Time of Preparation:

1 lb. smoked sausage, sliced into 1" slices

28-oz. can diced tomatoes, undrained

1 onion, chopped

½ cup sliced green bell pepper

1 Tbsp. sugar

1 tsp. paprika

½ tsp. dried thyme

½ tsp. dried oregano

¼ tsp. garlic powder

3 drops hot pepper sauce

Preparation Instructions:

1. Place all ingredients in a freezer bag and smoosh around.

2. Seal the bag, removing as much air as possible, then label it.

3. Place the freezer bag into a circular container that is slightly smaller than the diameter of your Instant Pot inner pot and freeze.

Information for Freezer Bag:

JIFFY JAMBALAYA

Makes 6 servings
Cook Time: 10 minutes

Needed at Time of Cooking:

1 cup chicken stock

3 cups cooked rice

Instructions:

1. Pour the stock and contents of the freezer bag into the inner pot of the Instant Pot.

2. Secure the lid and set the vent to sealing. Manually set the cook time for 10 minutes on high pressure.

3. When cook time is up, let the pressure release naturally for 5 minutes, then manually release the remaining pressure.

4. Remove the lid, stir in the rice, and serve.

BBQ Pork Sandwiches

Carol Eveleth, Cheyenne, WY

Makes 4 servings
Prep. Time: 20 minutes

Needed at Time of Preparation:

2-lb. pork shoulder roast, cut into 1" cubes

1 tsp. olive oil

2 tsp. salt

⅛ tsp. pepper

1 tsp. onion powder

1 tsp. garlic powder

Preparation Instructions:

1. Place all ingredients in a freezer bag and smoosh around to coat the pork pieces evenly.

2. Seal the bag, removing as much air as possible, then label it.

3. Place the freezer bag into a circular container that is slightly smaller than the diameter of your Instant Pot inner pot and freeze.

Information for Freezer Bag:

BBQ PORK SANDWICHES

Makes 4 servings
Cook Time: 15 minutes plus 3–5 minutes

Needed at Time of Cooking:

1 cup chicken or beef stock

2 cups barbecue sauce

Sandwich rolls or buns

Instructions:

1. Pour the stock and contents of the freezer bag into the inner pot of the Instant Pot.

2. Secure the lid and set vent to sealing. Manually set the cook time for 45 minutes on high pressure.

3. When cook time is up, let the pressure release naturally.

4. Remove the pork; shred it with two forks in a bowl.

5. Remove the liquid from the inner pot and discard.

6. Switch the Instant Pot to the Sauté function, then place the shredded pork and barbecue sauce in the inner pot. Simmer 3 to 5 minutes, stirring frequently.

7. Pile the shredded BBQ pork on the bottom half of a bun. Add any additional toppings if you wish, then finish with the top half of the bun.

Meatless Main Dishes

Eggplant Parmesan Lightened Up

Hope Comerford, Clinton Township MI

Makes 4 servings
Prep. Time: 25–30 minutes

Needed at Time of Preparation:

1 large eggplant

Salt

Nonstick cooking spray

2 cups low-sodium, low-sugar marinara
sauce, divided

½ tsp. dried basil

¾ cup shredded Parmesan cheese

Preparation Instructions:

1. Prepare the eggplant by cutting the top and bottom off, then slicing it in long ¼"-thick slices. Lay them out on a baking sheet and sprinkle them with salt on both sides. Let them sit for a few minutes and then pat each side dry with paper towel.

2. Spray a 7" springform or round baking pan with nonstick cooking spray.

3. Spread about ½ cup of marinara sauce on the bottom of the pan.

4. Begin layering your eggplant, a little marinara sauce, a sprinkle of basil, and a sprinkle of Parmesan until you have no more eggplant. End with sauce, a final sprinkle of basil, and Parmesan.

5. Wrap the pan tightly with several layers of plastic cling wrap, gently pushing the plastic wrap down so it is flesh with the top of the eggplant casserole, then wrap again with a couple layers of aluminum foil.

6. Label the foil and freeze.

EGGPLANT PARMESAN LIGHTENED UP

Makes 4 servings

Cook Time: 15 minutes ❧ *Cooling Time: 15–20 minutes*

Needed at Time of Cooking:

1 cup water

Serving Suggestion: Serve this alongside your favorite cooked pasta.

Instructions:

1. Remove the freezer wrapping of your Eggplant Parmesan. Recover the 7" pan with just aluminum foil.

2. Pour the water into the inner pot of the Instant Pot and place the trivet on top. Place the foil-covered pan on top of the trivet.

3. Secure the lid and set the vent to sealing. Manually set the cook time to 10 minutes on high pressure.

4. When cook time is up, manually release the pressure.

5. Remove the lid and carefully remove the trivet with oven mitts. Uncover the pan and allow the eggplant Parmesan to cool for about 15–20 minutes before serving.

Moroccan Spiced Sweet Potato Medley

Pat Bishop, Bedminster, PA

Makes 6 main-dish servings
Prep. Time: 45 minutes

Needed at Time of Preparation:

Salt

2 medium (about 1½ lb.) sweet potatoes, peeled and cut into ½" thick slices

1 medium onion, sliced

2 cloves garlic, crushed

1½ tsp. ground coriander

1½ tsp. ground cumin

¼ tsp. ground red pepper

14-oz. can stewed tomatoes, undrained

15-oz. can garbanzo beans, rinsed and drained

Preparation Instructions:

1. Set a pot ¾ of the way full of water, on the stove to boil. Add a bit of salt. When the water is boiling, add the sweet potato chunks and let them boil for 5 minutes. Drain the pot, then lay the potato chunks on some towels to dry and cool for about 30 minutes or so.

2. Add the cooled sweet potato chunks along with the remaining ingredients to a freezer bag.

3. Seal the bag, removing as much air as possible, then label it.

4. Place the freezer bag into a circular container that is slightly smaller than the diameter of your Instant Pot inner pot and freeze.

MOROCCAN SPICED SWEET POTATO MEDLEY

Makes 6 main-dish servings

Cook Time: 15 minutes

Needed at Time of Cooking/Serving:

2¼ cups water

2 cups cooked bulgur

½ cup dark raisins

1 cup loosely packed fresh cilantro leaves, chopped

Instructions:

1. Pour the water and contents of the freezer bag into the inner pot of the Instant Pot.

2. Secure the lid and set the vent to sealing. Manually set the cook time for 15 minutes on high pressure.

3. When cook time is up, manually release the pressure.

4. Remove the lid and stir in the cooked bulgur, raisins, and cilantro.

Vegetarian Coconut Curry

Hope Comerford, Clinton Township, MI

Makes 10–14 servings
Prep. Time: 15 minutes

Needed at Time of Preparation:

2 cups chopped broccoli florets

2 cups peeled and cubed butternut squash

I cup chopped carrots

¾ cup chopped onion

¾ cup chopped celery

½ cup chopped mushrooms

15½-oz. can garbanzo beans, drained and rinsed

½ cup vegetable stock

2 Tbsp. red curry paste

Preparation Instructions:

1. Place all ingredients in a freezer bag and smoosh around.

2. Seal the bag, removing as much air as possible, then label it.

3. Place the freezer bag into a circular container that is slightly smaller than the diameter of your Instant Pot inner pot and freeze.

Information for Freezer Bag:

VEGETARIAN COCONUT CURRY

Makes 10–14 servings
Cook Time: 4 minutes

Needed at Time of Cooking/Serving:

1 cup coconut milk

Cooked rice or pasta

Instructions:

1. Pour the coconut milk and contents of the freezer bag into the inner pot of the Instant Pot.

2. Secure the lid and set the vent to sealing. Manually set the cook time for 4 minutes on high pressure.

3. When cook time is up, manually release the pressure.

4. Stir and serve over cooked rice or pasta.

Lentil Tacos

Judy Buller, Bluffton, OH

Makes 6 servings
Prep. Time: 20 minutes

Needed at Time of Preparation:

¾ cup onions, finely chopped

⅛ tsp. garlic powder

½ lb. dry lentils, rinsed and picked clean of stones and floaters

1 Tbsp. chili powder

2 tsp. ground cumin

1 tsp. dried oregano

1 cup salsa

1 cup vegetable or chicken stock

Preparation Instructions:

1. Place all ingredients in a freezer bag.

2. Seal the bag, removing as much air as possible, then label it.

3. Place the freezer bag into a circular container that is slightly smaller than the diameter of your Instant Pot inner pot and freeze.

Information for Freezer Bag:

LENTIL TACOS

Makes 6 servings
Cook Time: 12 minutes

Needed at Time of Cooking/ Serving:

1 cup vegetable or chicken stock

12 taco shells

Optional toppings: shredded lettuce, tomatoes, chopped, shredded cheddar cheese, sour cream, taco sauce

Instructions:

1. Pour the stock and contents of the freezer bag into the inner pot of the Instant Pot.

2. Secure the lid and set the vent to sealing. Manually set the cook time for 12 minutes on high pressure.

3. When cook time is up, manually release the pressure.

4. Spoon about ¼ cup into each taco shell. Top with your choice of lettuce, tomatoes, cheese, sour cream, and taco sauce.

Lentils with Cheese

Kay Nussbaum, Salem, OR
Laura R. Showalter, Dayton, VA
Natalia Showalter, Mt. Solon, VA

Makes 6 servings
Prep. Time: 10 minutes

Needed at Time of Preparation:

1½ cups raw lentils, rinsed and picked clean of stones and floaters

½ tsp. salt

¼ tsp. pepper

⅛ tsp. dried marjoram

⅛ tsp. dried sage

⅛ tsp. dried thyme

2 large onions, chopped

2 cloves garlic, minced

14½-oz. can diced tomatoes

2 large carrots, sliced ⅛" thick

½ cup thinly sliced celery

1 bell pepper, chopped, *optional*

Vegetable broth

Preparation Instructions:

1. Place all ingredients into a gallon-size freezer bag.

2. Seal the bag, removing as much air as possible, then label it.

3. Place the freezer bag into a circular container that is slightly smaller than the diameter of your Instant Pot inner pot and freeze.

Information for Freezer Bag:

LENTILS WITH CHEESE

Makes 6 servings
Cook Time: 12 minutes

Needed at Time of Cooking:

2 cups water

1 cup (4 oz.) shredded cheddar cheese

Instructions:

1. Pour the water and contents of the freezer bag into the inner pot of the Instant Pot.

2. Secure the lid and set the vent to sealing. Manually set the cook time for 12 minutes on high pressure.

3. When cook time is up, manually release the pressure.

4. Remove the lid and stir in the shredded cheddar cheese.

BBQ Veggie Joes

Andrea Cunningham, Arlington, KS

Makes 10 servings
Prep. Time: 30 minutes

Needed at Time of Preparation:

I cup dried lentils, rinsed and picked
clean of stones and floaters

1½ cups chopped celery

1½ cups chopped carrots

I cup chopped onions

¾ cup ketchup

2 Tbsp. dark brown sugar

2 Tbsp. vegan Worcestershire sauce

I cup water

Preparation Instructions:

1. Place all ingredients in a freezer bag.

2. Seal the bag, removing as much air as possible, then label it.

3. Place the freezer bag into a circular container that is slightly smaller than the diameter of your Instant Pot inner pot and freeze.

Information for Freezer Bag:

BBQ VEGGIE JOES

Makes 10 servings
Cook Time: 12 minutes

Needed at Time of Cooking:

1 cup water

2 Tbsp. cider vinegar

10 sandwich rolls

Instructions:

1. Pour the water and contents of the freezer bag into the inner pot of the Instant Pot.

2. Secure the lid and set the vent to sealing. Manually set the cook time for 12 minutes on high pressure.

3. When cook time is up, manually release the pressure.

4. Stir in the vinegar just before serving.

5. Spoon ½ cup of lentil mixture onto each sandwich roll to serve.

Seafood Main Dishes

Shrimp Marinara

Jan Mast, Lancaster, PA

Makes 4–5 servings
Prep. Time: 5 minutes

Needed at Time of Preparation:

28-oz. can diced tomatoes

6-oz. can tomato paste

2 Tbsp. dried parsley

1 clove garlic, minced

¼ tsp. pepper

½ tsp. dried basil

1 tsp. dried oregano

½ tsp. salt

½ tsp. garlic salt

Preparation Instructions:

1. Place all ingredients in a freezer bag and smoosh around.

2. Seal the bag, removing as much air as possible, then label it.

3. Place the freezer bag into a circular container that is slightly smaller than the diameter of your Instant Pot inner pot and freeze.

Information for Freezer Bag:

SHRIMP MARINARA

Makes 4–5 servings
Cook Time: 7 minutes plus 4 minutes

Needed at Time of Cooking/ Serving:

1 cup vegetable or chicken stock

1 lb. fresh shrimp, peeled and deveined

Cooked spaghetti

Grated Parmesan cheese, *optional*

Instructions:

1. Pour the stock and contents of the freezer bag into the inner pot of the Instant Pot.

2. Secure the lid and set the vent to sealing. Manually set the cook time for 7 minutes.

3. When cook time is up, manually release the pressure.

4. Remove the lid and stir in the shrimp. Replace the lid, but do not lock it. Leave the lid on for 4 minutes, allowing the shrimp to cook.

5. Serve the shrimp marinara over the cooked spaghetti and garnish with the optional Parmesan cheese.

Lemon Dijon Orange Roughy

June S. Groff, Denver, PA

Makes 4 servings
Prep. Time: 10 minutes

Needed at Time of Preparation:

4 (5- or 6-oz.) orange roughy fillets

2 Tbsp. Dijon mustard

1 tsp. Worcestershire sauce

1 Tbsp. lemon juice

4 Tbsp. butter, *divided*

Preparation Instructions:

1. Lay each orange roughy fillet on a sheet of aluminum foil lined with parchment paper.

2. Mix together the mustard, Worcestershire sauce, and lemon juice in a small bowl, then spread it evenly on the 4 fillets.

3. Top each fillet with 1 Tbsp. of butter.

4. Close the foil packets tightly and place them into a freezer bag.

5. Seal the bag, removing as much air as possible, then label it. Freeze.

Information for Freezer Bag:

LEMON DIJON ORANGE ROUGHY

Makes 4 servings
Cook Time: 2 minutes

Needed at Time of Cooking:

1 cup water

Serving Suggestion: Serve with a baked potato and salad.

Instructions:

1. Pour the water into the bottom of the inner pot of the Instant Pot and place the trivet on top.

2. Unwrap each fillet and arrange them into a single layer in a 7" round baking pan. Place the pan on top of the trivet in the inner pot.

3. Secure the lid and set the vent to sealing. Manually set the cook time for 2 minutes on low pressure.

4. When cook time is up, manually release the pressure.

Herbed Fish Fillets

Patricia Howard, Green Valley, AZ

Makes 4 servings
Prep. Time: 10 minutes

Needed at Time of Preparation:

4 fish fillets (hake, cod, or mahi-mahi),
fresh or frozen

Juice of ½ lemon

1 tsp. dill weed

1 tsp. dried basil

1 tsp. no-salt seasoning

1 ½ tsp. parsley flakes

4 thin slices lemon

Preparation Instructions:

1. Lay each fillet on a sheet of aluminum foil lined with parchment paper.

2. In a small bowl, mix the lemon juice, dill, basil, no-salt seasoning and parsley. Pour this evenly over the fillets and place a slice of lemon on top of each fillet as well.

3. Close the foil packets tightly and place them in a freezer bag.

4. Seal the bag, removing as much air as possible, then label it. Freeze.

Information for Freezer Bag:

HERBED FISH FILLETS

Makes 4 servings
Cook Time: 9 minutes

Needed at Time of Cooking:

1 cup water

Serving Suggestion: Serve with a baked potato and salad.

Instructions:

1. Pour 1 cup of water into the inner pot of the Instant Pot and place the trivet on top.

2. Unwrap each fillet and arrange them into a single layer in a 7" round baking pan. Place the pan on top of the trivet in the inner pot.

3. Secure the lid and set the vent to sealing. Manually set the cook time for 9 minutes on high pressure.

4. When cook time is up, manually release the pressure.

Honey Lemon Garlic Salmon

Judy Gascho, Woodburn, OR

Makes 4 servings
Prep. Time: 10 minutes

Needed at Time of Preparation:

4 4-oz. fresh salmon filets

4 Tbsp. olive oil

3 Tbsp. honey

2–3 Tbsp. lemon juice

3 cloves garlic, minced

Salt to taste

Pepper to taste

1–2 Tbsp. minced parsley (dried or fresh)

Lemon slices, *optional*

Preparation Instructions:

1. Lay each fillet on a sheet of aluminum foil lined with parchment paper.

2. Mix olive oil, honey, lemon juice, and minced garlic in a bowl.

3. Brush each fillet generously with the olive oil mixture.

4. Sprinkle with salt, pepper, and parsley flakes.

5. Top each with a thin slice of lemon, if desired.

6. Close the foil packets tightly and place them in a freezer bag.

7. Seal the bag, removing as much air as possible, then label it. Freeze.

Information for Freezer Bag:

HONEY LEMON GARLIC SALMON

Makes 4 servings
Cook Time: 2 minutes

Needed at Time of Cooking:

1 cup water

Serving Suggestion: Serve with green beans and panfried potatoes.

Instructions:

1. Pour 1 cup of water into the inner pot of the Instant Pot and place the trivet on top.

2. Unwrap each fillet and arrange them into a single layer in a 7" round baking pan sprayed with nonstick cooking spray. Place the pan on top of the trivet in the inner pot.

3. Secure the lid and set the vent to sealing. Manually set the cook time for 2 minutes on low pressure.

4. When cook time is up, manually release the pressure.

Maple-Glazed Salmon

Jenelle Miller, Marion, SD

Makes 4 servings
Prep. Time: 10 minutes

Needed at Time of Preparation:

4 4-oz. salmon fillets

2 tsp. paprika

2 tsp. chili powder

½ tsp. ground cumin

½ tsp. brown sugar

½ tsp. kosher salt

Preparation Instructions:

1. Lay each fillet on a sheet of aluminum foil lined with parchment paper.

2. Combine the paprika, chili powder, cumin, brown sugar, and salt in a small bowl. Rub the fillets with seasoning mixture.

3. Close the foil packets tightly and place them in a freezer bag.

4. Seal the bag, removing as much air as possible, then label it. Freeze.

Information for Freezer Bag:

MAPLE-GLAZED SALMON

Makes 4 servings
Cook Time: 2 minutes

Needed at Time of Cooking:

1 cup water

1 Tbsp. maple syrup

Serving Suggestion: Serve with asparagus and a baked potato.

Instructions:

1. Pour 1 cup of water into the inner pot of the Instant Pot and place the trivet on top.

2. Unwrap each fillet and arrange them skin-side down in a 7" round baking pan. Pour the maple syrup over the top of the fillets. Place the pan on top of the trivet in the inner pot.

3. Secure the lid and set the vent to sealing. Manually set the cook time for 2 minutes on low pressure.

4. When cook time is up, manually release the pressure.

Caesar Salmon Fillets

Gloria D. Good, Harrisonburg, VA

Makes 4 servings
Prep. Time: 8 minutes

Needed at Time of Preparation:

4 4-oz. salmon fillets

½ cup fat-free Caesar salad dressing

1½ Tbsp. reduced-sodium soy sauce or tamari

1 clove garlic, minced

Preparation Instructions:

1. Lay each fillet on a sheet of aluminum foil lined with parchment paper.

2. Combine Caesar salad dressing, soy or tamari sauce, and minced garlic in a small bowl. Coat each fillet with this mixture.

3. Close the foil packets tightly and place them in a freezer bag.

4. Seal the bag, removing as much air as possible, then label it. Freeze.

Information for Freezer Bag:

CAESAR SALMON FILLETS

Makes 4 servings
Cook Time: 2 minutes

Needed at Time of Cooking:

1 cup water

Serving Suggestion: Serve with warm rolls and a Caesar salad.

Instructions:

1. Pour 1 cup of water into the inner pot of the Instant Pot and place the trivet on top.

2. Unwrap each fillet and arrange them skin-side down in a 7" round baking pan. Place the pan on top of the trivet in the inner pot.

3. Secure the lid and set the vent to sealing. Manually set the cook time for 2 minutes on low pressure.

4. When cook time is up, manually release the pressure.

Soups, Stews & Chilies

Chicken Vegetable Soup

Maria Shevlin, Sicklerville, NJ

Makes 6 servings
Prep. Time: 15 minutes

Needed at Time of Preparation:

1–2 raw chicken breasts, cubed

½ medium onion, chopped

4 cloves garlic, minced

½ sweet potato, small cubes

1 large carrot, peeled and sliced into rounds

4 stalks celery, chopped, leaves included

14½-oz. can petite diced tomatoes

1 tsp. salt

½ tsp. black pepper

1 tsp. garlic powder

¼ cup chopped fresh parsley

¼–½ tsp. red pepper flakes

Preparation Instructions:

1. Place all ingredients in a freezer bag and smoosh around.

2. Seal the bag, removing as much air as possible, then label it.

3. Place the freezer bag into a circular container that is slightly smaller than the diameter of your Instant Pot inner pot and freeze.

Information for Freezer Bag:

CHICKEN VEGETABLE SOUP

Makes 6 servings
Cook Time: 7 minutes

Needed at Time of Cooking:

3 cups chicken bone broth

½ cup frozen corn

¼ cup frozen peas

¼ cup frozen lima beans

1 cup frozen green beans (bite-sized)

¼–½ cup chopped savoy cabbage

Instructions:

1. Add the broth, corn, peas, lima beans, green beans, cabbage, and contents of the freezer bag to the inner pot of the Instant Pot.

2. Secure the lid and set the vent to sealing. Manually set the cook time for 7 minutes on high pressure.

3. When cook time is up, let the pressure release naturally for 5 minutes, then manually release the remaining pressure.

Spicy Chicken Soup with Edamame

J. B. Miller, Indianapolis, IN

Makes 8 servings
Prep. Time: 10 minutes

Needed at Time of Preparation:

1 ½ lb. boneless, skinless, chicken breasts, cut into 2" chunks

1 tsp. olive oil

1 bunch (about 6) green onions, thinly sliced

1 red bell pepper, chopped

1 yellow bell pepper, chopped

2 jalapeño peppers, seeded and finely chopped

4 cloves garlic, chopped

½ tsp. ground ginger

½ tsp. ground pepper

Preparation Instructions:

1. Place all ingredients in a freezer bag and smoosh around.

2. Seal the bag, removing as much air as possible, then label it.

3. Place the freezer bag into a circular container that is slightly smaller than the diameter of your Instant Pot inner pot and freeze.

Information for Freezer Bag:

SPICY CHICKEN SOUP WITH EDAMAME

Makes 8 servings
Cook Time: 18 minutes plus 5 minutes

Needed at Time of Cooking:

4 cups low-sodium chicken broth

3 cups fresh, or frozen, edamame, shelled

Instructions:

1. Add the broth and contents of the freezer bag to the inner pot of the Instant Pot.

2. Secure the lid and set the vent to sealing. Manually set the cook time for 18 minutes on high pressure.

3. When cook time is up, manually release the pressure.

4. Remove the lid, then remove the chicken and shred it between two forks. Replace it back in the soup.

5. Stir the edamame into the soup and press Keep Warm. Allow it to cook for about 5 additional minutes, then serve.

Chicken Cheddar Broccoli Soup

Maria Shevlin, Sicklerville, NJ

Makes 4–6 servings
Prep. Time: 10 minutes

Needed at Time of Preparation:

1 lb. raw chicken breast, chopped into bite-sized pieces

1 lb. fresh broccoli, chopped

½ cup onion, chopped

2 cloves garlic, minced

1 cup shredded carrots

½ cup finely chopped celery

¼ cup finely chopped red bell pepper

½ tsp. salt

¼ tsp. black pepper

½ tsp. garlic powder

1 tsp. parsley flakes

Pinch red pepper flakes

Preparation Instructions:

1. Place all ingredients in a freezer bag and smoosh around.

2. Seal the bag, removing as much air as possible, then label it.

3. Place the freezer bag into a circular container that is slightly smaller than the diameter of your Instant Pot inner pot and freeze.

Information for Freezer Bag:

CHICKEN CHEDDAR BROCCOLI SOUP

Makes 4–6 servings
Cook Time: 18 minutes plus 5 minutes

Needed at Time of Cooking:

3 cups chicken bone broth

2 cups heavy cream

8 oz. freshly shredded cheddar cheese

2 Tbsp. Frank's RedHot Original Cayenne Pepper Sauce

Serving suggestion: Serve it up with slice or two of keto garlic bread or bread of your choice.

Instructions:

1. Pour the broth and contents of the freezer bag into the inner pot of the Instant Pot.

2. Secure the lid and make sure vent is at sealing. Manually set the cook time for 18 minutes on high pressure.

3. Manually release the pressure when cook time us up, remove lid, and stir in heavy cream.

4. Place pot on sauté setting until it all comes to a low boil, approximately 5 minutes.

5. Stir in cheese and the hot sauce. Turn off the pot and stir until cheese is melted.

White Chicken Chili

Judy Gascho, Woodburn, OR

Makes 6 servings
Prep. Time: 10 minutes

Needed at Time of Preparation:

1½–2 lb. boneless chicken breasts or thighs, cut into 1½" chunks

1 medium onion, chopped

3 cloves garlic, minced

3 15-oz. cans great northern beans, undrained

15-oz. can white corn, drained

4½-oz. can chopped green chilies, undrained

1 tsp. cumin

½ tsp. ground oregano

Preparation Instructions:

1. Place all ingredients in a freezer bag and smoosh around.

2. Seal the bag, removing as much air as possible, then label it.

3. Place the freezer bag into a circular container that is slightly smaller than the diameter of your Instant Pot inner pot and freeze.

Information for Freezer Bag:

WHITE CHICKEN CHILI

Makes 6 servings
Cook Time: 8 minutes

Needed at Time of Cooking:

2 cups chicken broth

1 cup sour cream

1½ cups grated cheddar or Mexican blend cheese

Serving suggestion: Delicious served with chopped cilantro and additional cheese.

Instructions:

1. Pour the broth and contents of the freezer bag into the inner pot of the Instant Pot.

2. Secure the lid and set the vent to sealing. Manually set the cook time for 8 minutes on high pressure.

3. When cook time is up, let the pressure release naturally for 10 minutes, then manually release the remaining pressure.

4. Remove chicken and shred it.

5. Put chicken, sour cream, and cheese in the inner pot. Stir until cheese is melted.

Turkey Chili

Reita F. Yoder, Carlsbad, NM

Makes 8 servings
Prep. Time: 10 minutes

Needed at Time of Preparation:

2 lb. ground turkey, browned and
cooled

1 medium onion, chopped

1 clove garlic, minced

16-oz. can pinto, or kidney, beans

2 14-oz. cans diced chopped tomatoes

15-oz. can tomato sauce

1-oz. pkg. chili seasoning

Preparation Instructions:

1. Place all ingredients in a freezer bag and smoosh around.

2. Seal the bag, removing as much air as possible, then label it.

3. Place the freezer bag into a circular container that is slightly smaller than the diameter of your Instant Pot inner pot and freeze.

Information for Freezer Bag:

TURKEY CHILI

Makes 8 servings
Cook Time: 7 minutes

Needed at Time of Cooking:

1½ cups chicken stock

Serving Suggestion: Serve with corn bread.

Instructions:

1. Pour the stock and contents of the freezer bag into the inner pot of the Instant Pot.

2. Secure the lid and set the vent to sealing. Manually set the cook time for 7 minutes on high pressure.

3. When cook time is up, let the pressure release naturally for 10 minutes, then manually release the remaining pressure.

Ground Turkey Stew

Carol Eveleth, Cheyenne, WY

Makes 4–6 servings

Prep. Time: 10 minutes

Needed at Time of Preparation:

I lb. ground turkey, browned and cooled

I onion, chopped

½ tsp. garlic powder

I tsp. chili powder

¾ tsp. cumin

2 tsp. coriander

I tsp. dried oregano

½ tsp. salt

I green pepper, chopped

I red pepper, chopped

14-oz. can diced tomatoes

I ½ cups tomato sauce

I Tbsp. soy sauce

Preparation Instructions:

1. Place all ingredients in a freezer bag and smoosh around.

2. Seal the bag, removing as much air as possible, then label it.

3. Place the freezer bag into a circular container that is slightly smaller than the diameter of your Instant Pot inner pot and freeze.

Information for Freezer Bag:

GROUND TURKEY STEW

Makes 4–6 servings

Cook Time: 7 minutes plus 5 minutes

Needed at Time of Cooking:

1 cup water

2 handfuls cilantro, chopped

15-oz. can black beans

Instructions:

1. Pour the water and contents of the freezer bag into the inner pot of the Instant Pot.

2. Secure the lid and make sure the vent is set to sealing. Manually set the cook time for 7 minutes on high pressure.

3. When cook time is up, let the pressure release naturally for 10 minutes, then manually release any remaining pressure.

4. Remove the lid. Switch the Instant Pot to the Sauté function and add the cilantro and can of black beans. Combine well, and let cook for about 5 minutes.

Instantly Good Beef Stew

Hope Comerford, Clinton Township, MI

Makes 6 servings
Prep. Time: 10 minutes

Needed at Time of Preparation:

2 lb. stewing beef, cubed

2 cloves garlic, minced

1 large onion, chopped

3 ribs celery, chopped

2–3 carrots, sliced

8 oz. tomato sauce

2 tsp. Worcestershire sauce

¼ tsp. pepper

1 bay leaf

Preparation Instructions:

1. Place all ingredients in a freezer bag and smoosh around.

2. Seal the bag, removing as much air as possible, then label it.

3. Place the freezer bag into a circular container that is slightly smaller than the diameter of your Instant Pot inner pot and freeze.

Information for Freezer Bag:

INSTANTLY GOOD BEEF STEW

Makes 6 servings
Cook Time: 35 minutes

Needed at Time of Cooking:

1½ cups beef stock

3 large potatoes, cubed

Serving Suggestion: Serve with buttered crusty bread.

Instructions:

1. Pour the beef stock, potatoes, and contents of the freezer bag into the inner pot of the Instant Pot.

2. Secure the lid and set the vent to sealing. Manually set the cook time for 35 minutes.

3. When cook time is up, let the pressure release naturally.

4. Remove the lid, discard the bay leaf, then serve.

Tuscan Beef Stew

Karen Ceneviva, Seymour, CT

Makes 8 servings
Prep. Time: 5–10 minutes

Needed at Time of Preparation:

2 lb. stewing beef, cut into 1" cubes

10½-oz. can tomato soup

1 tsp. Italian seasoning

½ tsp. garlic powder

14½-oz can Italian diced tomatoes

¾ lb. carrots, cut into 1" chunks

2 15½-oz. cans cannellini beans, rinsed and drained

Preparation Instructions:

1. Place all ingredients in a freezer bag and smoosh around.

2. Seal the bag, removing as much air as possible, then label it.

3. Place the freezer bag into a circular container that is slightly smaller than the diameter of your Instant Pot inner pot and freeze.

Information for Freezer Bag:

TUSCAN BEEF STEW

Makes 8 servings
Cook Time: 20 minutes

Needed at Time of Cooking:

1 cup beef broth

¼ cup water

Instructions:

1. Pour the broth, water, and contents of the freezer bag into the inner pot of the Instant Pot.

2. Secure the lid and set the vent to sealing. Manually set the cook time for 20 minutes on high pressure.

3. When cook time is up, let the pressure release naturally.

Nancy's Vegetable Beef Soup

Nancy Graves, Manhattan, KS

Makes 8 servings
Prep. Time: 5 minutes

Needed at Time of Preparation:

2-lb. roast, cubed, or 2 lb. stewing meat

15-oz. can corn

15-oz. can green beans

40-oz. stewed tomatoes

1½ Tbsp. beef bouillon powder

Tabasco to taste

½ tsp. salt

Preparation Instructions:

1. Place all ingredients in a freezer bag. Do not drain the vegetables.

2. Seal the bag, removing as much air as possible, then label it.

3. Place the freezer bag into a circular container that is slightly smaller than the diameter of your Instant Pot inner pot and freeze.

Information for Freezer Bag:

NANCY'S VEGETABLE BEEF SOUP

Makes 8 servings
Cook Time: 20 minutes

Needed at Time of Cooking:

1-lb. bag frozen peas

Water to fill line

Instructions:

1. Empty the contents of the freezer bag, along with the peas, into the inner pot of the Instant Pot. Pour water in only until you reach the fill line.

2. Secure the lid and set the vent to sealing. Manually set the cook time for 20 minutes on high pressure.

3. When cook time is up, let the pressure release naturally.

Tomato Beef Soup

Hope Comerford, Clinton Township, MI

Makes 6 servings
Prep. Time: 10 minutes

Needed at Time of Preparation:

1 lb. 95%-lean ground beef, browned and cooled

1 small onion, chopped

2 cloves garlic, chopped

2 Tbsp. tomato paste

2 14½-oz. cans diced tomatoes

2 carrots, sliced

1 chopped green, or red, bell pepper

1 tsp. Italian seasoning, *optional*

½ tsp. salt

⅛ tsp. black pepper

Preparation Instructions:

1. Place all ingredients in a freezer bag and smoosh around.

2. Seal the bag, removing as much air as possible, then label it.

3. Place the freezer bag into a circular container that is slightly smaller than the diameter of your Instant Pot inner pot and freeze.

Information for Freezer Bag:

TOMATO BEEF SOUP

Makes 6 servings
Cook Time: 13 minutes

Needed at Time of Cooking:

4 cups beef stock

1 large potato, diced

Instructions:

1. Pour the beef stock, diced potato, and contents of the freezer bag into the inner pot of the Instant Pot.

2. Secure the lid and set the vent to sealing. Manually set the cook time for 13 minutes on high pressure.

3. When cook time is up, let the pressure release naturally for 5 minutes, then release the remaining pressure manually.

Favorite Chili

Carol Eveleth, Cheyenne, WY

Makes 4–6 servings
Prep. Time: 10 minutes

Needed at Time of Preparation:

1 lb. ground beef, browned and cooled

1 small onion, chopped

2 cloves garlic, minced

1 green pepper, chopped

2 Tbsp. chili powder

1 tsp. salt

½ tsp. cumin

½ tsp. black pepper

16-oz. can chili beans, undrained

15-oz. can crushed tomatoes

Preparation Instructions:

1. Place all ingredients in a freezer bag and smoosh around.

2. Seal the bag, removing as much air as possible, then label it.

3. Place the freezer bag into a circular container that is slightly smaller than the diameter of your Instant Pot inner pot and freeze.

Information for Freezer Bag:

FAVORITE CHILI

Makes 4–6 servings
Cook Time: 15 minutes

Needed at Time of Cooking:

1 cup water

Instructions:

1. Pour the water and contents of the freezer bag into the inner pot of the Instant Pot.

2. Secure the lid and make sure the vent is set to sealing. Manually set the cook time for 15 minutes on high pressure.

3. When cook time is up, let the pressure release naturally.

Beef and Black Bean Chili

Eileen B. Jarvis, St. Augustine, FL

Makes 8 servings
Prep. Time:10 minutes

Needed at Time of Preparation:

1 lb. 95%-lean ground beef, browned and cooled

1 small onion, chopped

2 (15-oz.) cans black beans, rinsed and drained

1 cup medium, or hot, chunky salsa

16-oz. can tomato sauce

1 Tbsp. chili powder

Preparation Instructions:

1. Place all ingredients in a freezer bag and smoosh around.

2. Seal the bag, removing as much air as possible, then label it.

3. Place the freezer bag into a circular container that is slightly smaller than the diameter of your Instant Pot inner pot and freeze.

Information for Freezer Bag:

CHICKEN VEGETABLE SOUP

Makes 8 servings
Cook Time: 7 minutes

Needed at Time of Cooking/Serving:

1 cup water or beef stock

Low-fat sour cream, *optional*

Reduced-fat shredded cheddar cheese, *optional*

Instructions:

1. Pour the water or stock and contents of the freezer bag into the inner pot of the Instant Pot.

2. Secure the lid and set the vent to sealing. Manually set the cook time for 7 minutes on high pressure.

3. When cook time is up, let the pressure release naturally for 5 minutes, then manually release the remaining pressure.

4. When serving, if you wish, top individual servings with sour cream and/or a sprinkle of reduced-fat shredded cheddar cheese.

Italian Vegetable Soup

Patti Boston, Newark, OH

Makes 6 servings
Prep. Time: 20 minutes

Needed at Time of Preparation:

3 small carrots, sliced

1 small onion, chopped

2 Tbsp. chopped parsley

1 clove garlic, minced

3 tsp. beef bouillon powder

1¼ tsp. dried basil

¼ tsp. pepper

16-oz. can red kidney beans, undrained

14½-oz. can stewed tomatoes, with juice

1 cup diced, extra-lean, cooked ham

Preparation Instructions:

1. Place all ingredients in a freezer bag and smoosh around.

2. Seal the bag, removing as much air as possible, then label it.

3. Place the freezer bag into a circular container that is slightly smaller than the diameter of your Instant Pot inner pot and freeze.

Information for Freezer Bag:

ITALIAN VEGETABLE SOUP

Makes 6 servings
Cook Time: 8 minutes

Needed at Time of Cooking:

2 small potatoes, diced

3 cups water

Instructions:

1. Place the potatoes, water, and contents of the freezer bag into the inner pot of the Instant Pot.

2. Secure the lid and set the vent to sealing. Manually set the cook time for 8 minutes on high pressure.

3. When cook time is up, let the pressure release naturally.

Napa Cabbage and Pork Soup

Shirley Unternahrer, Wayland, IA

Makes 8 servings
Prep. Time: 10 minutes

Needed at Time of Preparation:

1 lb. lean ground pork* (not sausage),
browned and cooled

1 small onion, chopped

2 Tbsp. fish sauce (found in Asian foods
section)

½ tsp. turbinado sugar, or sugar of your
choice

Preparation Instructions:

1. Place all ingredients in a freezer bag and smoosh around.

2. Seal the bag, removing as much air as possible, then label it.

3. Place the freezer bag into a circular container that is slightly smaller than the diameter of your Instant Pot inner pot and freeze.

Information for Freezer Bag:

NAPA CABBAGE AND PORK SOUP

Makes 8 servings
Cook Time: 20 minutes

Needed at Time of Cooking/ Serving:

4 cups low-sodium chicken stock

1 head (about 8 cups) napa cabbage, shredded

6 green onions, chopped

Instructions:

1. Pour the chicken stock, cabbage, and contents of the freezer bag into the inner pot of the Instant Pot.

2. Secure the lid and set the vent to sealing. Manually set the cook time for 20 minutes on high pressure.

3. When cook time is up, let the pressure release naturally.

4. When serving, top each bowl with a sprinkling of green onions.

Split Pea Soup

Judy Gascho, Woodburn, OR

Makes 3–4 servings
Prep. Time: 20 minutes

Needed at Time of Preparation:

4 oz. ham, diced (about ⅓ cup)

4 sprigs thyme

2 Tbsp. butter

2 carrots, peeled and cut into rounds

1 large leek, chopped

3 cloves garlic

1½ cups dried green split peas (about 12 oz.), sorted and rinsed

1 cup chicken broth

Preparation Instructions:

1. Place all ingredients in a freezer bag and smoosh around.

2. Seal the bag, removing as much air as possible, then label it.

3. Place the freezer bag into a circular container that is slightly smaller than the diameter of your Instant Pot inner pot and freeze.

Information for Freezer Bag:

SPLIT PEA SOUP

Makes 3–4 servings
Cook Time: 15 minutes

Needed at Time of Cooking/ Serving:

2 stalks celery, chopped

3 cups chicken broth

Salt to taste

Pepper to taste

Instructions:

1. Place the celery, broth, and contents of the freezer bag into the inner pot of the Instant Pot.

2. Secure the lid and set the vent to sealing. Manually set the cook time for 15 minutes on high pressure.

3. When the time is up, let the pressure release naturally.

4. Remove the lid and stir the soup; discard the thyme sprigs.

5. Thin the soup with up to 1 cup water if needed (the soup will continue to thicken as it cools). Season with salt and pepper.

French Market Soup

Ethel Mumaw, Berlin, OH

Makes 8 servings (about 2½ qts. total)
Prep. Time: 20 minutes

Needed at Time of Preparation:

1 ham hock, all visible fat removed

1 tsp. salt

¼ tsp. pepper

16-oz. can low-sodium tomatoes

1 large onion, chopped

1 clove garlic, minced

1 chili pepper, chopped, or 1 teaspoon chili powder

¼ cup lemon juice

1 cup water

2 cups mixed dry beans, washed, with stones removed

Preparation Instructions:

1. Combine all ingredients, except the beans, in a freezer bag and smoosh around.

2. Place the freezer bag into a circular container that is slightly smaller than the diameter of your Instant Pot inner pot and add the beans on top.

3. Seal the bag, removing as much air as possible, then label it. Freeze.

Information for Freezer Bag:

FRENCH MARKET SOUP

Makes 8 servings (about 2½ quarts total)
Cook Time: 30 minutes

Needed at Time of Cooking:

5 cups water

Instructions:

1. Pour the water into the inner pot of the Instant Pot and invert the contents of the freezer bag on top so the beans are at the bottom of the pot.

2. Secure the lid and make sure vent is set to sealing. Manually set the cook time for 30 minutes on high pressure.

3. When cook time is up, let the pressure release naturally.

4. Remove the lid, then remove the bone and any hard or fatty pieces from the ham hock. Pull the meat off the bone and chop it into small pieces. Add the ham back into the Instant Pot.

Ham and Bean Soup

Susie Nisley Millersburg, OH

Makes 10 servings
Prep. Time: 10 minutes

Needed at Time of Preparation:

1 lb. extra-lean ham, diced

1 lb. dry navy beans, rinsed

1 small onion, chopped

1 green bell pepper, diced

½ carrot, diced

1 cup tomato juice

2 tsp. garlic powder

½ tsp. cumin

½ tsp. black pepper

1 tsp. no-salt seasoning

Preparation Instructions:

1. Place all the ingredients in a freezer bag.

2. Seal the bag, removing as much air as possible, then label it.

3. Place the freezer bag into a circular container that is slightly smaller than the diameter of your Instant Pot inner pot and freeze.

Information for Freezer Bag:

HAM AND BEAN SOUP

Makes 10 servings
Cook Time: 30 minutes

Needed at Time of Cooking/ Serving:

7 cups reduced-sodium chicken stock

1 bunch fresh cilantro, chopped

Instructions:

1. Pour the stock and contents of the freezer bag into the inner pot of your Instant Pot.

2. Secure the lid and set the vent to sealing. Manually set the cook time for 30 minutes on high pressure.

3. When cook time is up, let the pressure release naturally.

4. Before serving, stir in the chopped fresh cilantro.

Potato Bacon Soup

Colleen Heatwole, Burton, MI

Makes 4–6 servings
Prep. Time: 30 minutes

Needed at Time of Preparation:

Salt

5 lb. potatoes, peeled and cubed

3 stalks celery, diced into roughly
¼- to ½" pieces

1 large onion, chopped

1 clove garlic, minced

1 Tbsp. seasoning salt

½ tsp. black pepper

1 cup chicken broth

1 lb. bacon, fried crisp and rough
chopped

Preparation Instructions:

1. Set a large pot on the stove with salted water and bring to a boil. Add the potatoes to the water and let them boil for 2–3 minutes. Remove and lay them on a towel to dry and cool.

2. Once the potatoes are cooled, add them to a freezer bag along with the remaining ingredients.

3. Seal the bag, removing as much air as possible, then label it.

4. Place the freezer bag into a circular container that is slightly smaller than the diameter of your Instant Pot inner pot and freeze.

Information for Freezer Bag:

POTATO BACON SOUP

Makes 4–6 servings
Cook Time: 8 minutes

Needed at Time of Cooking/ Serving:

3 cups chicken broth

1 cup half-and-half

1 cup milk, 2% or whole

Optional sour cream, shredded cheddar cheese, and diced green onion to garnish

Instructions:

1. Pour the broth and contents of the freezer bag into the inner pot of the Instant Pot.

2. Secure the lid and set the vent to sealing. Manually set the cook time for 8 minutes on high pressure.

3. When cook time is up, let the pressure release naturally.

4. Remove the lid. Roughly mash the potatoes, leaving some large chunks if desired.

5. Add the half-and-half and milk, stirring constantly.

6. Serve while still hot with desired assortment of garnishes.

Green Bean and Ham Soup

Carla Keslowsky, Hillsboro, KS

Makes 4 servings
Prep. Time: 5 minutes

Needed at Time of Preparation:

1 ham hock

1 medium onion, chopped

1 sprig fresh dill weed

16-oz. pkg. frozen green beans, or 1 lb. fresh beans

½ tsp. black pepper

Preparation Instructions:

1. Place all ingredients in a freezer bag.

2. Seal the bag, removing as much air as possible, then label it.

3. Place the freezer bag into a circular container that is slightly smaller than the diameter of your Instant Pot inner pot and freeze.

Information for Freezer Bag:

GREEN BEAN AND HAM SOUP

Makes 4 servings
Cook Time: 8 minutes plus 5 minutes

Needed at Time of Cooking:

2 potatoes, peeled and cubed

7½ cups water or reduced-sodium chicken stock

½ cup nonfat milk

Instructions:

1. Place the potatoes and contents of the freezer bag into the inner pot of the Instant Pot and add the water or stock.

2. Secure the lid and set the vent to sealing. Manually set the cook time for 8 minutes on high pressure.

3. When cook time is up, let the pressure release naturally.

4. Remove the lid and then remove the ham hock and hard fatty pieces. Separate the meat from the bone. Discard the bone and stir the ham meat back into the soup.

5. Slowly stir in the milk. Let it heat through and serve.

Pork Chili

Carol Duree, Salina, KS

Makes 5 servings
Prep. Time: 10 minutes

Needed at Time of Preparation:

1 lb. boneless pork ribs, cut into
1" chunks

2 14½-oz. cans fire-roasted diced
tomatoes

4¼-oz. cans diced green chili peppers,
drained

½ cup chopped onion

1 clove garlic, minced

1 tablespoon chili powder

Preparation Instructions:

1. Place all the ingredients in a freezer bag.

2. Seal the bag, removing as much air as possible, then label it.

3. Place the freezer bag into a circular container that is slightly smaller than the diameter of your Instant Pot inner pot and freeze.

Information for Freezer Bag:

PORK CHILI

Makes 5 servings
Cook Time: 25 minutes

Needed at Time of Cooking:

1 cup chicken stock

Instructions:

1. Pour the stock and contents of the freezer bag into the inner pot of the Instant Pot.

2. Secure the lid and set the vent to sealing. Manually set the cook time for 25 minutes on high pressure.

3. When cook time is up, let the pressure release naturally for 10 minutes, then manually release any remaining pressure.

4. Remove the lid and then remove the pork chunks. Shred the meat. Stir it back through the chili and serve.

White Bean Soup

Esther H. Becker, Gordonville, PA

Makes 6 servings
Prep. Time: 5 minutes

Needed at Time of Preparation:

8 oz. (about 1¼ cups) dried white beans, rinsed

1 cup low-fat, low-sodium chicken stock

1 tsp. grapeseed or olive oil

1 onion, diced

2 cups diced raw sweet potatoes (about 2 medium potatoes)

1 cup diced green bell pepper

¼ tsp. ground cloves

¼ tsp. pepper

½ tsp. dried thyme

Preparation Instructions:

1. Place all ingredients in a freezer bag.

2. Seal the bag, removing as much air as possible, then label it.

3. Place the freezer bag into a circular container that is slightly smaller than the diameter of your Instant Pot inner pot and freeze.

Information for Freezer Bag:

WHITE BEAN SOUP

Makes 6 servings
Cook Time: 40 minutes

Needed at Time of Cooking:

2 cups low-fat, low-sodium chicken stock

4 cups water

½ cup low-sugar ketchup

¼ cup molasses

Instructions:

1. Pour the contents of the freezer bag into the inner pot of the Instant Pot, along with the stock and water.

2. Secure the lid and set the vent to sealing. Manually set the cook time for 40 minutes on high pressure.

3. When cook time is up, allow the pressure to release naturally for 10 minutes, then manually release the remaining pressure.

4. Remove the lid and stir in the ketchup and molasses. Add more water if you would like your soup to be thinner.

Black Bean Soup

Colleen Heatwole, Burton, MI

Makes 4–6 servings
Prep. Time: 10 minutes

Needed at Time of Preparation:

1 cup coarsely chopped onion

2 cups dry black beans, cleaned of debris and rinsed

1 tsp. olive oil

1 cup vegetable or chicken broth

3 cloves garlic, minced

½ tsp. paprika

⅛ tsp. red pepper flakes

2 large bay leaves

1 tsp. cumin

2 tsp. oregano

½ tsp. salt (more if desired)

Preparation Instructions:

1. Place all ingredients in a freezer bag.

2. Seal the bag, removing as much air as possible, then label it.

3. Place the freezer bag into a circular container that is slightly smaller than the diameter of your Instant Pot inner pot and freeze.

Information for Freezer Bag:

BLACK BEAN SOUP

Makes 4–6 servings
Cook Time: 40 minutes

Needed at Time of Cooking/ Serving:

5 cups vegetable or chicken broth

Yogurt or sour cream for garnish, *optional*

Instructions:

1. Pour the broth and contents of the freezer bag into the inner pot of the Instant Pot.

2. Secure the lid and set the vent to sealing. Manually set the cook time for 40 minutes on high pressure.

3. When cook time is up, let pressure release naturally for 10 minutes, then manually release the remaining pressure.

4. Open the lid. Remove the bay leaves and discard them. Serve with desired garnishes.

Brown Lentil Soup

Colleen Heatwole, Burton, MI

Makes 3–5 servings
Prep. Time: 15 minutes

Needed at Time of Preparation:

1 lb. brown lentils, rinsed and picked clean of stones and floaters

1 medium onion, chopped

1 medium carrot, chopped

2 cloves garlic, minced

1 small bay leaf

1 cup chicken broth

Preparation Instructions:

1. Place all ingredients in a freezer bag.

2. Seal the bag, removing as much air as possible, then label it.

3. Place the freezer bag into a circular container that is slightly smaller than the diameter of your Instant Pot inner pot and freeze.

Information for Freezer Bag:

BROWN LENTIL SOUP

Makes 3–5 servings
Cook Time: 15 minutes

Needed at Time of Cooking:

4 cups chicken broth

1 tsp. salt

¼ tsp. ground black pepper

½ tsp. lemon juice

Instructions:

1. Pour the chicken broth and contents of the freezer bag into the inner pot of the Instant Pot.

2. Secure the lid and make sure the vent is set to sealing. Manually set the cook time for 15 minutes on high pressure.

3. When cook time is up, let the pressure release naturally.

4. Remove the lid and discard the bay leaf.

5. Stir in the salt, pepper, and lemon juice, then serve.

Sweet Potato Soup with Kale

Hope Comerford, Clinton Township, MI

Makes 8 servings
Prep. Time: 10 minutes

Needed at Time of Preparation:

Salt

2 lb. sweet potatoes, peeled and diced

1 medium onion, chopped

2 cloves garlic, chopped

14½-oz can diced tomatoes

1 bay leaf

1 tsp. paprika

½ tsp. coriander

1 sprig fresh rosemary

¼ tsp. pepper

1 cup reduced-sodium chicken or
vegetable stock

Preparation Instructions:

1. Set a large pot on the stove with salted water and bring to a boil. Add the potatoes to the water and let them boil for 2–3 minutes. Remove and lay them on a towel to dry and cool.

2. Place the cooled potatoes and all the remaining ingredients in a freezer bag.

3. Seal the bag, removing as much air as possible, then label it.

4. Place the freezer bag into a circular container that is slightly smaller than the diameter of your Instant Pot inner pot and freeze.

Information for Freezer Bag:

SWEET POTATO SOUP WITH KALE

Makes 8 servings
Cook Time: 10 minutes plus 3–5 minutes

Needed at Time of Cooking:

4 cups reduced-sodium chicken or
vegetable stock

5 oz. chopped kale

Instructions:

1. Pour the stock and contents of the freezer bag into the inner pot of the Instant Pot.

2. Secure the lid and set the vent to sealing. Manually set the cook time for 10 minutes on high pressure.

3. When cook time is up, let the pressure release naturally for 10 minutes, then manually release the remaining pressure.

4. Remove the lid and gently stir the kale into the soup. Let the soup sit for a few minutes so the kale can wilt, then serve.

Butternut Squash Soup

Colleen Heatwole, Burton, MI

Makes 4 servings
Prep. Time: 20 minutes

Needed at Time of Preparation:

2 large butternut squash, peeled,
seeded, and cut into 1" cubes
(about 4 lb.)

1 cup chicken stock

2 Tbsp. butter

1 large onion, chopped

2 cloves garlic, minced

1 tsp. thyme

½ tsp. sage

Salt to taste

Pepper to taste

Preparation Instructions:

1. Place all ingredients in a freezer bag.

2. Seal the bag, removing as much air as possible, then label it.

3. Place the freezer bag into a circular container that is slightly smaller than the diameter of your Instant Pot inner pot and freeze.

Information for Freezer Bag:

BUTTERNUT SQUASH SOUP

Makes 4 servings
Cook Time: 8 minutes

Needed at Time of Cooking:

3 cups chicken stock

Instructions:

1. Pour the chicken stock and contents of the freezer bag into the inner pot of your Instant Pot.

2. Secure the lid and set the vent to sealing. Manually set the cook time for 8 minutes on high pressure.

3. When cook time is up, let the pressure release naturally.

4. Remove the lid. Puree the soup in a food processor or use immersion blender right in the inner pot. If soup is too thick, add more stock. Adjust salt and pepper as needed.

Potato and Spinach Soup

Jane S. Lippincott, Wynnewood, PA

Makes 6 servings
Prep. Time: 30 minutes

Needed at Time of Preparation:

Salt

4 medium russet potatoes, unpeeled and chopped into 1" thick pieces

2 ribs celery, chopped

1 medium onion, chopped

1 clove garlic, minced

1 tsp. mustard seeds

¼ tsp. pepper

1 cup chicken or vegetable stock

Preparation Instructions:

1. Set a large pot on the stove with salted water and bring to a boil. Add the potatoes to the water and let them boil for 2–3 minutes. Remove and lay them on a towel to dry and cool.

2. Place the cooled potatoes and all the remaining ingredients in a freezer bag.

3. Seal the bag, removing as much air as possible, then label it.

4. Place the freezer bag into a circular container that is slightly smaller than the diameter of your Instant Pot inner pot and freeze.

Information for Freezer Bag:

POTATO AND SPINACH SOUP

Makes 6 servings
Cook Time: 8 minutes plus 10 minutes

Needed at Time of Cooking/ Serving:

3 cups chicken or vegetable stock

6 cups chopped fresh spinach

1 Tbsp. white wine vinegar

Chopped chives for garnish

Instructions:

1. Pour the stock and contents of the freezer bag into the inner pot of the Instant Pot.

2. Secure the lid and set the vent to sealing. Manually set the cook time for 8 minutes on high pressure.

3. When cook time is up, let the pressure release naturally.

4. Remove the lid. Use a potato masher to mash the mixture a bit.

5. Stir in the chopped spinach and vinegar. Press Sauté and let the soup simmer uncovered for 10 minutes more.

6. Serve with chives sprinkled on top of individual servings.

Flavorful Tomato Soup

Shari Ladd, Hudson, MI

Makes 4 servings
Prep. Time: 5 minutes

Needed at Time of Preparation:

2 Tbsp. chopped onions

1 qt. stewed tomatoes, no salt added,

2 tsp. turbinado sugar

½ tsp. pepper

¼ tsp. dried basil

½ tsp. dried oregano

¼ tsp. dried thyme

Preparation Instructions:

1. Place all ingredients in a freezer bag.

2. Seal the bag, removing as much air as possible, then label it.

3. Place the freezer bag into a circular container that is slightly smaller than the diameter of your Instant Pot inner pot and freeze.

Information for Freezer Bag:

FLAVORFUL TOMATO SOUP

Makes 4 servings
Cook Time: 5 minutes

Needed at Time of Cooking:

1 cup chicken or vegetable stock

6 Tbsp. butter

3 Tbsp. flour

2 cups skim milk

Instructions:

1. Pour the stock and contents of the freezer bag into the inner pot of the Instant Pot.

2. Secure the lid and set the vent to sealing. Manually set the cook time for 5 minutes on high pressure.

3. When cook time is up, let the pressure release naturally for 10 minutes, then manually release the remaining pressure.

4. While the pressure is releasing, in a small pot on the stove, melt the butter. Once the butter is melted, whisk in the flour and cook for 2 minutes, whisking constantly. Slowly whisk the skim milk into the pot.

5. Remove the lid of the Instant Pot. Slowly whisk the milk/butter/flour mixture into the tomato soup.

6. Use an immersion blender to puree the soup.

Three-Bean Chili

Chris Kaczynski, Schenectady, NY

Makes 6 servings
Prep. Time: 10 minutes

Needed at Time of Preparation:

1 medium onion, diced

16-oz. can low-sodium red kidney beans, drained

16-oz. can low-sodium black beans, drained

16-oz. can low-sodium white kidney, or garbanzo, beans, drained

14-oz. can low-sodium crushed tomatoes

14-oz can low-sodium diced tomatoes

1 cup medium salsa

1 pkg. dry chili seasoning

1 Tbsp. sugar

Preparation Instructions:

1. Place all ingredients in a gallon-size freezer bag.

2. Seal the bag, removing as much air as possible, then label it.

3. Place the freezer bag into a circular container that is slightly smaller than the diameter of your Instant Pot inner pot and freeze.

Information for Freezer Bag:

THREE-BEAN CHILI

Makes 6 servings
Cook Time: 5 minutes

Needed at Time of Cooking:

1 cup vegetable stock

Instructions:

1. Pour the stock and contents of the freezer bag into the inner pot of the Instant Pot.

2. Secure the lid and set the vent to sealing. Manually set the cook time for 5 minutes on high pressure.

3. When cook time is up, let the pressure release naturally for 10 minutes, then manually release the remaining pressure.

Metric Equivalent Measurements

If you're accustomed to using metric measurements, I don't want you to be inconvenienced by the imperial measurements I use in this book.

Weight (Dry Ingredients)

1 oz		30 g
4 oz	¼ lb	120 g
8 oz	½ lb	240 g
12 oz	¾ lb	360 g
16 oz	1 lb	480 g
32 oz	2 lb	960 g

Volume (Liquid Ingredients)

½ tsp.		2 ml
1 tsp.		5 ml
1 Tbsp.	½ fl oz	15 ml
2 Tbsp.	1 fl oz	30 ml
¼ cup	2 fl oz	60 ml
⅓ cup	3 fl oz	80 ml
½ cup	4 fl oz	120 ml
⅔ cup	5 fl oz	160 ml
¾ cup	6 fl oz	180 ml
1 cup	8 fl oz	240 ml
1 pt	16 fl oz	480 ml
1 qt	32 fl oz	960 ml

Length

¼ in	6 mm
½ in	13 mm
¾ in	19 mm
1 in	25 mm
6 in	15 cm
12 in	30 cm

Recipe and Ingredient Index

About the Author

Hope Comerford is a mom, wife, elementary music teacher, blogger, recipe developer, public speaker, Young Living Essential Oils essential oil enthusiast/educator, and published author. In 2013, she was diagnosed with a severe gluten intolerance and since then has spent many hours creating easy, practical, and delicious gluten-free recipes that can be enjoyed by both those who are affected by gluten and those who are not.

Growing up, Hope spent many hours in the kitchen with her Meme (grandmother), and her love for cooking grew from there. While working on her master's degree when her daughter was young, Hope turned to her slow cookers for some salvation and sanity. It was from there she began truly experimenting with recipes and quickly learned she had the ability to get a little more creative in the kitchen and develop her own recipes.

In 2010, Hope started her blog, *A Busy Mom's Slow Cooker Adventures*, to simply share the recipes she was making with her family and friends. She never imagined people all over the world would begin visiting her page and sharing her recipes with others as well. In 2013, Hope self-published her first cookbook, *Slow Cooker Recipes 10 Ingredients or Less and Gluten-Free*, and then later wrote *The Gluten-Free Slow Cooker*.

Hope became the new brand ambassador and author of Fix-It and Forget-It in mid-2016. Since then, she has brought her excitement and creativeness to the Fix-It and Forget-It brand. Through Fix-It and Forget-It, she has written *Fix-It and Forget-It Healthy Slow Cooker Cookbook*, *Fix-It and Forget-It Healthy 5-Ingredient Cookbook*, *Fix-It and Forget-It Instant Pot Cookbook*, *Fix-It and Forget-It Plant-Based Comfort Foods Cookbook*, *Welcome Home Harvest Cookbook*, *Welcome Home Pies, Crisps, and Crumbles*, and many more.

Hope lives in the city of Clinton Township, Michigan, near Metro Detroit. She has been happily married to her husband and best friend, Justin, since 2008. Together they have two children, Ella and Gavin, who are her motivation, inspiration, and heart. In her spare time, Hope enjoys traveling, singing, cooking, reading books, working on wooden puzzles, spending time with friends and family, and relaxing.